365

NATURE
Crafts & Activities

Karen E. Bledsoe
Candyce Norvell

Consultant:
Nancy Goodman

Illustrators:
Terri and Joe Chicko

Publications International, Ltd.

Editorial Assistance: Susan Milord, Kelly Boyer Sagert
Illustrations: Terri and Joe Chicko
Cover Photography: Brian Warling
Models: Royal Model Management: Andrea Kolarits,
Thurston Magill
Stylist: Mary Beth Janssen
Crafter: Lynette Schuepbach

Karen E. Bledsoe holds masters degrees in teaching
and science. She currently lectures in biology at Western Oregon State University. She has served as environ-
mental educator and recreational leader for the City of
Salem (Ore.) Parks and Recreation and worked as a
biological technician at Mt. Hood National Forest.

Candyce Norvell is a freelance writer who has
authored and edited numerous texts for elementary to
high school students. Her work has appeared in publications such as *Seventeen, ym,* and *Campus Voice.* She
currently serves as editorial director for a series of activ
ities books for middle school students.

Nancy Goodman has a Master of Science in biological
science. Currently a freelance writer and editor, she
has developed curriculum for the Chicago Children's
Museum and the Museum of Science and Industry. She
has written and edited textbooks for numerous educa-
tional publishers and has served as assistant director of
education at the Chicago Botanic Garden.

CONTENTS

ART FROM NATURE

Nature is all around us—in the woods, in the desert, in the middle of a city, even in the air. Have you looked closely at the trees that grow along city streets, or weeds coming up through cracks in the pavement? Have you watched butterflies and other insects flying on the warm summer air? Or birds dining at a bird feeder? They are all part of nature.

You don't have to be an expert to enjoy the beauty of the outdoors. All you need is the spirit of adventure on any scale. Do you enjoy getting out for a hike in the mountains or a walk in the woods? Maybe you like gardening or growing houseplants. Or perhaps you simply like watching birds or butterflies from your window.

Nature is everywhere for you to see, but it does charge for admission. Its secrets are revealed only to those who are willing to open their eyes and ears, to touch and smell—and sometimes even taste! In return, nature offers the excitement of discovery, the joy of beauty, and the thrill of learning about the things that interest you the most.

Nature will most willingly share its gifts with those who are responsible in taking care of them. Always use care when you do the projects in this book. When you gather materials from nature, take only what you need. Never take so much of any one thing that you leave a "scar." Never let it be obvious that you've been collecting materials.

Be sure to observe local laws before you gather materials outdoors. Get permission from property owners. Never collect from state forests—or from city, state, or national parks. Find out what rare plants and animals live in your area and be certain not to disturb them.

When you see wild animals, sit back and enjoy them. See how much you can learn simply by observing. What do they eat? Where do they live? Can you spot the edges of an animal's territory? Never chase them or try to catch them (except insects, and then only for a few minutes to study up close). Almost all mammals bite and scratch to defend themselves. Many reptiles will bite, too, though few are poisonous. Birds will peck. No animal enjoys being caught and some will even die of fright. Remember that state and federal laws protect most wild animals from harm.

Be courteous to plants, too. Many of us like to pick flowers to bring indoors, but it's better to leave wild flowers for others to enjoy. A flower is a plant's way of making seeds so it can reproduce. Leave the flower in place and come back later to see what kind of seeds it made. If you like to bring flowers indoors, grow some in a garden just for cutting.

When you think about protecting plants and wildlife, think beyond the individuals. Scientists, foresters, and land managers today are working to protect entire habitats. Many animals and plants are endangered because they are losing their homes—their habitats. Many of the projects in this book are designed to help you show your concern about protecting nature's resources.

In addition to practicing responsibility, you must practice safety when you are outdoors. Know how to recognize poison oak, poison ivy, or poison sumac, whichever grows in your area. Know how to recognize poisonous snakes, and stay away from them. Many newts and salamanders secrete a strong poison, so avoid handling them.

When you go hiking, always go with adults. Stay on the trails to avoid getting lost and to protect the fragile soil. Wear bright colors. Bring rain gear and clean water. Carry a whistle to signal others if you should get separated from your group. Obey all signs, particularly signs warning you about potential dangers. Never feed the animals, no matter how cute

they look. White bread, corn curls, and other junk people like to feed animals aren't good for them. If animals store junk food in their food supply, it usually rots and spoils the rest of the food. Then the animals starve in the winter.

When you look through the projects in this book, notice the number of "leaves" by them. These show how difficult the project is. Simple projects have one leaf, medium projects have two, and challenging projects have three. You should be able to do the simple projects yourself. You may want to ask for help on the harder ones. Some projects also have a caution. These projects may involved flames, sharp blades, or other hazards. Get an adult to help you with them.

Simple   *Medium*   *Challenging*

Before starting any project in this book, ask an adult for permission. You want to be certain which household materials you can use. Also ask where you can gather the materials you need. Adults often have good ideas to help you complete your projects.

Feel free to experiment with these projects. You may have your own ideas about how you want your craft to look. That's all right. Go ahead and make it your own.

Most of all, be sure to have fun!

OUR PRECIOUS PLANET

Dirt, wonderful dirt—and rocks and sand are all elements we love to dig into. Plants need dirt to grow in; animals make their homes there. So what is dirt? In this chapter you'll learn about soil, how it's made, and what's in it. You'll discover rocks and minerals, and have fun with sand. You'll find out that there's a lot more beneath our feet than you thought!

WHAT A RELIEF!

very area of the Earth has high places and low places. A relief map is a pecial kind of map that shows these highs and lows.

What You'll Need: Plywood, plaster of Paris or modeling clay, paints

Whether it's your backyard or the whole United States, you'll find high and low points. A relief map is ke a small model showing mountains, hills, and valleys. You can make a relief map on a piece of plywood. First, draw an outline of the area you're going to map. Then use plaster of Paris or modeling clay to fill in the outline. Pile up the clay to show the high places! If you're mapping a large area, such as the state you live in, you'll need to look at a map that shows mountains and valleys. If you're mapping a small area such as your backyard, just map what you see. After your map dries, paint it. Use different colors to highlight the highs and lows. For example, you could paint the highest mountaintops white like snow, and the valleys green like plants.

BE A ROCK HOUND

2

Is it igneous or metamorphic? You'll find out when you create your very own rock collection.

What You'll Need: Rocks, rock identifying books, box

No matter where you live, there are rocks around. But what *kind* of rocks depend on what part of the country you live in. In some regions, there are (literally) tons of granite lying around. In other regions, most of the rock is sandstone or limestone.

The kinds of rocks you find in a region depend on what kinds of minerals are found there. (Rocks are made out of minerals.) It also depends on what geologic "events" have happened in the area. For example, if a volcano ever dumped molten lava in your area, you'll find lots of *igneous* rocks. If your region was once under water, you'll find *sedimentary* rocks (rocks made when mud, sand, and minerals settle and harden). And if the Earth has buckled, you'll find *metamorphic* rocks (rocks that have been changed by pressure and/or heat). These are the three basic kinds of rocks. All rocks fall into one of these three types.

Take a hike through your neighborhood and see how many different kinds of rocks you can find. Look along roads, streams, lakes, and excavations for rocks of different colors and different textures (smooth or rough, shiny or dull). But be careful!

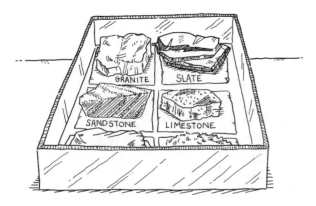

Then see if you can identify your rocks. One way to identify rocks is to use a book that shows the different kinds. Check out a book from your library, and match your rock samples to pictures and descriptions in the book. The book will probably also tell you what minerals are in each kind of rock, and how it was formed. Another way is to go to a rock shop. There you'll see samples of all different kinds of rocks, labeled with their names. Which ones look like rocks you found?

Keep expanding your rock collection as you find new and unusual rocks. Keep your rock collection in a box. You can glue each rock to the box and label it, or make a compartment for samples of each kind of rock.

A ROCKIN' RECIPE

3

All rocks are made of minerals that have been combined by heat and pressure. You can make some edible "rocks" to show how this happens.

What You'll Need: Large marshmallows, butter or margarine, pan, waxed paper, nuts, raisins, or chocolate chips, puffed rice, large spoon, rock identifying book

With help from your parents or an adult, melt 40 marshmallows and three tablespoons of butter or margarine in a pan, stirring them together. Measure out onto waxed paper about one cup of each of the following: nuts (any kind you like), raisins, or chocolate chips.

Stir the six cups of puffed rice cereal into the melted marshmallows and butter. Then use a big spoon to drop "hunks" of the mixture onto waxed paper. Let it cool just a little, until you can handle it without burning yourself. Be careful when handling this hot mixture!

Coat your hands with butter. Then make rocks by combining the ingredients of your choice with the cereal/marshmallow mix. The melted marshmallows provide the heat. You provide the pressure. And you can make different kinds of "rocks" depending on which 'minerals' you add. Look in a rock identifying book to compare your rocks to real rocks. Did you make granite, marble, or perhaps something else?

Your rocks, of course, are a little different than nature's rocks. For one thing, yours will taste better!

ELEMENTARY SCIENCE

Just eight simple elements make up 98 percent of the rocks in the world today. What eight elements do you think they might be? If you guessed oxygen, silicon, aluminum, iron, calcium, sodium, potassium, and magnesium, then take a bow—because you're right!

POWERFUL PLANTS

4

You might think that rocks would be stronger than plants. But plants are strong enough to break through rock when they have to.

What You'll Need: Beans, water, bowl, plaster of Paris, an aluminum-foil baking pan

Soak a handful of beans in water overnight. Pour plaster of Paris into an aluminum foil baking pan. The plaster of Paris should be a couple of inches deep. Sprinkle the soaked beans on top. Cover the beans with another layer of plaster of Paris that is about an inch thick. Watch what happens. When the beans sprout, they will break right through the rocklike plaster of Paris.

You can see examples of this in nature. When you go for a walk, look for plants and trees growing up through rock. Or you might see tree roots breaking up a concrete sidewalk.

BE A SCULPTOR

5

Try your hand at sculpting the animals that live in your neighborhood. Who knows? You may discover a hidden talent.

What You'll Need: Plaster of Paris, half-gallon milk cartons, sculpting tools or dull knife

For as long as there have been people and rocks, people have used rocks to make sculptures. For example, the Inuit people of the Arctic carve polar bears and seals from a kind of rock called soapstone. Here's how you can create your own masterpiece.

Fill two or more half-gallon milk cartons with plaster of Paris. Give them plenty of time to dry completely. Then strip off the milk cartons. You'll have blocks of plaster of Paris that you can sculpt. Use some simple sculpting tools, which you can get at a hobby or art store, or a dull knife. You may want to draw the shape of your animal on the plaster of Paris before you begin sculpting. Begin with a simple animal such as a fish or a seal.

MAKING AN IMPRESSION

6

Leave your mark on the world (or at least on plaster) when you create your own "fossils."

What You'll Need: Small natural object (shell, leaf, bone, etc.), petroleum jelly, plaster of Paris, water, small disposable dish (such as a margarine tub)

Fossils are imprints of plants and animals found in rocks. Here is one way fossils are made in nature: A leaf falls into wet, sandy ground. A flood deposits more sandy soil on top of the leaf, so that it is trapped there. Over thousands of years, the leaf decays and disappears. But as the sandy soil hardens into rock, the impression made by the leaf is left in the rock. You can see how fossils are created by making your own.

First, choose an object to make a fossil of. It could be a shell, a leaf, an animal bone, or another object from nature. Coat the object with petroleum jelly. Next, pour some plaster of Paris and some water in a small dish. Mix them together well. Let the plaster of Paris and water sit for a few minutes, without stirring them. Press the object into the plaster of Paris and let everything dry. This will take at least one day. When the plaster of Paris is completely dry, remove the object. The impression left behind is like a fossil.

DINOSAUR FOSSILS

Believe it or not, people didn't know about ancient animals, such as reptiles and dinosaurs, in 1811. Then, in England, a 12-year-old girl named Mary Anning went out searching for sea shells. While she may have found some beautiful shells, she also found a huge fossil—with just about all the bones still in place! Scientists decided to name this fossil an *Ichthyosaurus*, a long word that means "fish-lizard." Her discovery led others to search for more fossil skeletons.

PEBBLE SCULPTURES

All it takes is a little imagination to turn your ordinary pebbles into extraordinary art.

What You'll Need: Pebbles, thick glue, poster paint or acrylic paint, brushes

If you have a collection of ordinary rocks that you don't know what to do with, try making sculptures from them. Lay out your rocks and look for interesting features that might suggest faces, animal heads, arms, legs, or bodies. A large, smooth rock might make you think of a beetle. A heart-shaped rock could be part of a pebble valentine. Glue the rocks together with thick, sticky glue. (Hot glue works best, but have an adult help you with the hot glue gun.) Use acrylic paints or poster paints to paint your figures. Decorate your rocks with other natural things you find. An acorn cap makes a good hat. Feathers that you pick up can become tails for your pebble birds. White thistledown or cotton from cottonwoods can make white Santa Claus beards and hair. Give your dog or cat a good brushing and use the hair that comes out as hair for your pebble people. Find a discarded board with a large knothole and put your pebble mice or owls in the hole.

A FLOATING ROCK

Most rocks sink in water, but do you know which rock can actually float on water? The answer is pumice, a stone that was once volcanic lava. Pumice has lots of little holes in it that were formed by bubbles in the lava. The holes contain air, which keeps the rock afloat!

PEBBLE MOSAIC

8

You've probably seen magnificent mosaic decorations made from glass and stone in a church or museum. Now you can make your own version from pebbles!

What You'll Need: Plywood or particle board, craft glue or tile grout, a variety of pebbles

After you've collected lots of pretty pebbles in different colors and shapes, you can use them to make your mosaic. If you like, first use a pencil to draw a design on a piece of plywood. Then glue the pebbles on the design. Or, spread the plywood with grout, and push the pebbles into the grout.

A pebble mosaic makes a good trivet (used to hold hot pots). You can also make pebble mosaics to decorate flower pots, vases, or lamps. What else could you decorate with pebbles?

PRECIOUS JEWELS

9

Surprise someone you know with a special present—jewelry made from natural gems.

What You'll Need: Some interesting "found" stones, jewelry fittings available at a crafts store, craft glue

How many times have you been walking along, looked down, and seen a really interesting rock? You pick it up, explore it, and put it in your pocket. It's easy and fun to make those special rocks into jewelry for yourself or your friends and family. After all, gemstones are just minerals that have been cut into shapes and then polished. (Sapphires, for instance, are made from a mineral called corundum.) Crafts stores have all kinds of jewelry fittings. For example, they have pin backs—just glue one to the back of a special rock, and you have a beautiful pin. They also have glue-on fittings that you can use to make earrings, necklaces, bracelets, and rings.

10 ANCIENT MESSAGES

Paint rocks to create petroglyphs, just like people did in ancient times.

What You'll Need: Crumbly rocks or dirt, bag, hammer, binding medium (such as egg yolks, liquid soap, or liquid starch), large flat rock

"Petro" means rock and "glyph" means carving, so petroglyphs are rock carvings. Some ancient petroglyphs pointed the way to a stream or a shelter. Some might have told others, "Grog was here." These writings tell us about people who lived thousands of years ago.

Here's how to make your own petroglyphs:

First, make your paint. Use crumbly rocks, dirt, or a mixture of both. Whatever you use, it should be colorful so it will show up when you paint it on a flat rock. Crush the rocks into a powder. Put them in a grocery bag and pound them with a hammer. Mix the powder with egg yolks, liquid soap, or liquid starch.

Now use your fingers to make petroglyphs on a large, flat rock. What do you have to say to people who will live thousands of years from now?

11 GO FOR THE GOLD

You probably won't strike it rich gold panning, but it's fun to try!

What You'll Need: Gold pan or old pie tin, tweezers, small bottle, magnet, life vest

Most areas of the country have at least a few streams that have yielded gold. Ask at the local Forest Service or Bureau of Land Management office to find out where to go near you.

Never go near the water without an adult nearby. Also, don't go in water that is deeper than your knees. Find a spot in the stream where the bottom is sandy and without too many rocks. Scoop up a handful of sand with plenty of water in your pan and swirl it around. Let the lighter sand spill out over the edge of the pan. Heavier materials, including iron and gold, will remain behind. The heavy sand is darker in color, too.

When the darker sand is all you have left in the pan, pour out the water and look closely. If you're lucky you'll see small specks of gold gleaming in it. Use tweezers to pick the gold from the sand and put it in your bottle. Later, let the gold and sand dry. Use a magnet to lift away the iron-rich dark sand, leaving the gold.

WHAT STONE ARE YOU?

12

Were you born an amethyst, a peridot, or a zircon? Learn all about your special birthstone.

What You'll Need: Encyclopedia or rock identifying book, paper clay, tapestry needle, paint, paintbrush, string

In ancient times, each month was said to have a special stone. Over time, people came up with at least two stones for most months. That stone—or stones—supposedly brought good luck to people who were born in that month. For example, the stone for January is garnet, a red gem. People born in January wore jewelry made with garnets. These special stones became known as birthstones. Many people still wear their birthstones.

Find your birthstone on the following list. Learn as much about the stone as you can, including what it looks like and where it is found. Look up your stone in an encyclopedia or rock book. If you can, go to a rock shop so you can see your birthstone. Pay attention to the shape and color of your birthstone.

Using paper clay, create beads that resemble gemstones. Use a tapestry needle to make a hole in each bead. Let the beads dry overnight. Then paint the beads the same color as your birthstone. Since most stones have various shades, you may want to mix a few colors of paint together in order to get the right one. After the paint has dried, thread the beads on a short piece of string to make a bracelet or a long piece of string to make a necklace.

Month	Birthstone
January	garnet
February	amethyst
March	aquamarine or bloodstone
April	diamond
May	emerald or agate
June	pearl or moonstone
July	ruby or onyx
August	carnelian or peridot
September	sapphire or chrysolite
October	opal, beryl, or tourmaline
November	topaz
December	turquoise or zircon

MINERAL TESTING KIT

13

Super rock hounds will want to put together this simple kit for identifying minerals and testing their properties.

What You'll Need: Canvas or denim scraps, needle and thread, thick string, penny, small piece of glass, piece of unglazed tile, file or pocket knife, small bottle of vinegar, eyedropper, rocks, reference book about rocks

Make a small, sturdy bag to carry your kit in: Cut two 6-inch by 8-inch pieces of canvas or denim and put them together, wrong side out. Sew three sides together. Fold over one inch of fabric on the top. Sew together to form a casing. Slit one of the seams open in the casing and slip a drawstring through it.

Into the bag, put a penny, a small piece of glass, a piece of unglazed tile, a file or pocket knife, a small bottle of vinegar, and an eyedropper. Now use your kit to test rocks and minerals to help you identify them.

1. Use the tile to test the 'streak' of the mineral. Do this by scratching the tile with your rock and seeing what color the scratches are.

2. Vinegar is used to test for the presence of calcium carbonate. Put a drop of vinegar on the rock. If it fizzes, the rock contains calcium carbonate.

3. The rest of the items test for hardness, on a hardness scale of 1 to 10.

    1-2: fingernail can scratch rock

    3: penny can scratch rock

    4-5: knife blade or file can scratch rock

    6: glass can scratch rock

    7: rock can scratch knife or file; rock can barely scratch glass

    8-10: harder than common minerals

Use what you learn to identify the rocks in a reference book about rocks.

MAGNETIC MINERALS

14

Is there iron in your cereal? With a little help from science, you can perform some breakfast table magic.

What You'll Need: Cereal, plastic bag, rolling pin, strong magnet

The iron that your body needs to make healthy blood is the same iron that is found in the Earth. If the cereal you eat for breakfast is high in iron, it should be attracted to a magnet.

Put some cereal in a plastic bag and use a rolling pin to crush it into powder. Then, touch the magnet to the powder. Does the cereal cling to the magnet?

BE A MINERAL DETECTIVE

15

Calcium carbonate is one of the most common minerals in nature. See if you can discover some in your home.

What You'll Need: Wide-mouthed jar, vinegar, raw egg (in the shell), different kinds of chalk

Both eggshells and limestone contain calcium carbonate, and some chalk is made from it. It's simple to find out whether or not a substance has calcium carbonate in it. Simply drop a sample into a jar of vinegar. If the vinegar dissolves (or partly dissolves) the substance, it contains calcium carbonate.

To try this, fill a wide-mouthed jar with vinegar. Gently place a whole egg in the jar. Watch the eggshell begin to fizz. Over a couple of days, it will completely dissolve! That's because an eggshell is almost all calcium carbonate.

Try the same thing with several different chalk samples. If the chalk is made from calcium carbonate, it will fizz and at least partly dissolve. Some chalk is made from another mineral called gypsum, which will not fizz and dissolve in vinegar.

GROW A CRYSTAL "GARDEN"

16

At one time, these were called "Depression gardens" because they were an inexpensive project for children during the Great Depression of the 1930s.

What You'll Need: Chunks of coal, brick, flower pot pieces, or pieces of unglazed porcelain; old shallow bowls about 6 inches wide; mixing bowl; salt (not iodized); liquid bluing; water; ammonia; ink or food coloring in several colors

Remember to be careful when working with any broken objects and when pouring ammonia. Have an adult supervise this project.

Break coal, brick, clay flower pots, or unglazed porcelain into chunks the size of walnuts. Place several in an old dish, clustering them near the center. (Don't overcrowd the dish.) For each dish, mix four tablespoons of salt (not iodized), four tablespoons of liquid bluing, four tablespoons of water, and one tablespoon of household ammonia. Pour the mixture very slowly over the broken pieces in your dish. Drip food coloring on the pieces sticking up out of the solution. Set the bowl aside in a place it won't be disturbed. In a few hours you should see crystals "growing" in your garden.

To make crystal blossoms: Make a larger batch of the solution given above but leave out the ammonia. Make enough to completely cover the broken pieces in the dish (keep the pile low, under the rim of the dish). Add more solution every day or two to keep the same liquid level. After two weeks stop adding solution and allow the liquid to evaporate completely. Beautiful blossom shapes will form.

CRYSTAL CLEAR

Rocks are made up of minerals. As a mineral grows, it sometimes forms into beautiful shapes known as crystals. One common mineral is quartz, which is created by a combination of silicon and oxygen. Quartz often forms into a milky white, six-sided crystal. Another quartz crystal, called amethyst, turns into a wonderful shade of purple.

SWEET CRYSTALS

17

In this activity, you'll do two things at once: See how crystals form in nature, and make candy!

What You'll Need: Saucepan, water, sugar, glass jar, string, pencil, popsicle stick

With the help of an adult, boil half a cup of water in a saucepan. Add a cup of sugar one spoonful at a time until all the sugar is dissolved. Keep adding sugar until the solution turns into a clear syrup. Let it cool for about 10 minutes, then pour the syrup into a glass jar.

Now get a piece of string about six inches long. Tie one end of the string around a pencil, then tie the other end to a popsicle stick. Put the pencil on top of the jar so the popsicle stick hangs in the syrup.

Set your 'crystal maker' aside. Take a look at it every day to see what's happening. In about a week, the syrup should be crystallized and ready to eat.

DIAMONDS IN THE SAND

You can find sand on beaches, riverbeds, and deserts, but what is sand? Most sand is really tiny grains of quartz. In Hawaii, there are larger sizes of quartz grains that sparkle so much that they are called "diamonds." Sailors who landed in Hawaii in the early 1800s thought the shimmering grains of quartz really were diamonds. Sometimes pure quartz sand is even used to make glass.

18 CANDLES IN THE SAND

Light up the darkness with these decorative candles created from sand.

What You'll Need: Wax or old candles, pan or coffee can, cardboard box, sand, small candles

Sand, which is made of tiny grains of rock (usually quartz), has many uses. Bags full of sand keep rivers from jumping their banks and flooding the surrounding area. Sand sprinkled on icy sidewalks and roads can keep people and cars from slipping. Sand can even be used as a mold for making candles. Here's how:

With help from your parents or an adult, melt some wax (this is a good way to reuse old candles) in an old pan or an empty coffee can. Fill a box with damp sand. Use your fist to hollow out some holes in the sand. Put a small candle in the center of each hole. The candles' wicks should reach the tops of the holes. Finally, fill each hole around the small candle with melted wax. Be careful not to burn yourself with the hot wax! Let your candles sit overnight, then dig them out of the sand.

To make a candle with legs: Poke your finger down into the sand in three places after you have made your fist depression. You will have a flat-topped candle that stands on three wax legs.

NATURE'S CONCRETE 19

Make beautiful pottery and long-lasting sculptures with simple sand clay.

What You'll Need: Water, clean sand, cornstarch, pot or bowl

For thousands of years, people have mixed sand with other natural ingredients to make bricks, pots, and other things they need. You can do the same thing. With the help of a parent or adult, boil some water. For each cup of clean sand, mix ½ cup of cornstarch and ½ cup of boiling water in a sturdy pot or bowl. Stir the mixture several times as it cools.

Now, shape the mixture into pots and jars, or make sculptures of animals or other shapes. To harden the concrete, bake your creations in a 300°F oven for one hour. Let it cool completely before handling.

ART THE NAVAJO WAY

20

The Navajo people have made sand paintings for centuries.

What You'll Need: Colored sand, cardboard or poster board, pencil, newspapers, glue, water, paintbrush

Navajo sand paintings almost always show nature: trees, plants, animals, lightning, and other wonders. You can make your own nature sand painting. You'll need several colors of sand. You can collect sand from nature, or buy it at a crafts store. Then start with a piece of cardboard or poster board. Use a pencil to draw a nature picture. Set your poster board on plenty of old newspapers.

Now mix white glue half-and-half with water. Use a paintbrush to paint a thin, even layer of the glue-and-water mixture every place where you want one color of sand. Sprinkle sand over the painted areas. Let dry for a few minutes, then turn your picture over and tap off the extra sand. (Do this over a trash can!)

Repeat the process with the next color: Paint glue on all the areas that will be the same color. Sprinkle on the sand, let dry, and tap off. Repeat this until you've finished your sand painting.

PLAY WITH CLAY

21

There is natural clay all over the earth. See if you can find clay near you.

What You'll Need: A small shovel

Clay is soil that's made of very tiny bits of minerals and other elements. These tiny bits stick together, packing so close that they keep out water. That's what makes clay squishy and stretchy.

See if you can locate some natural clay where you live. Start by asking people who garden what they know about natural clay. They can tell you if there's a lot of it around. You'll have to dig for it—clay is usually under the topsoil. When you find something that you think might be clay, try rolling a piece of it into a ball. (You may need to add some water.) If it holds its shape, like modeling clay, it's clay. Clean all the rocks, leaves, twigs, and other debris out of the clay. Then use it to make a small pot. Pots made from natural clay aren't completely waterproof, but they can last a long time if you're careful with them.

IT'S NOT JUST DIRT

22

There's more to dirt than just dirt. Discover what's in the soil.

What You'll Need: Pie pan, garden soil, water

Fill a pie pan with soil collected from an outdoor garden. Bring the pie pan indoors, and place it where it gets sunlight. Keep the pie pan away from open windows, so nothing gets into the pan from outside. Water the soil to keep it moist. Observe the soil each day. Do you see any earthworms or tiny insects? Is anything sprouting or growing? When you're finished, put the soil and all its creatures back in the garden.

WASHED AWAY

23

Learn how erosion—when soil is washed away by wind or water—occurs.

What You'll Need: Three aluminum-foil cooking pans; three lengths of rubber or plastic tubing (½-inch in diameter); tape; a mixture of soil, sand, and clay; potting soil; blocks of wood; three bowls; cereal grains

Poke a small hole in one end of each aluminum pan, near the upper rim. Put one end of a length of tubing into each hole, using tape to hold it there. Into each pan put a layer of the soil, sand, and clay mixture. Then add a layer of potting soil on top of that. Put all three pans indoors in a place where they will get sunlight. Rest all three pans on blocks of wood to elevate the pans at about a 30-degree angle. The tubing should be on the bottom end of each pan. Put the free end of each tube into a bowl.

In one pan, make rows across the width of the pan and plant cereal grains in the rows. In another pan, make the rows lengthwise and plant the grain. Don't plant anything in the third pan. Use a plant mister to keep the grain moist until it sprouts. Continue to water the grain until the seedlings are about two inches tall. Don't do anything to the empty pan. Once the seedlings in the two pans are about two inches tall, begin using a watering can to sprinkle all three pans. The watering can should have a spout that imitates rain. Each time you water the pans, watch the water that runs into the bowls. Which bowl collects more potting soil? Why? What could you do to prevent potting soil from eroding into the bowls?

THAT SETTLES IT!

24

When soil, sand, and other materials settle at the bottom of a lake or pond it is called sediment. Over time, layers of sediment can form rock.

What You'll Need: Jar with lid, soil, sand, gravel, water, small plastic animals (optional)

Put a handful each of soil, sand, and gravel into a jar. Fill the jar with water. Put the lid on tightly. Shake the jar well until everything is mixed together. Now let the jar sit overnight. In the morning, see how the different things in the jar have settled. How would you describe what you see? What can you say about the layers? Compare your layers to what happens in a lake or pond.

If you want to see how fossilized critters are made, put small, plastic animals in with your soil, sand, and gravel mixture.

IT'S YOUR FAULT

25

A fault is a place where there is a break in the Earth's crust. You can use clay to make your own model of a fault.

What You'll Need: Three different colors of clay, a dull knife

Earthquakes often begin at a fault in the Earth. If rock near a fault suddenly begins to move, it creates pressure that causes an earthquake. Here's a simple way to show how it works:

Get three pieces of clay, each in a different color, and pound each piece into a flat rectangle. Stack them on top of one another and press them together. The three pieces of clay stand for layers of the Earth's crust.

Use a dull knife to cut all the way through the layers, in the middle. Put the two sections of clay together, but don't match them up exactly as they were before you cut them apart. The cut is like a fault in the Earth's crust.

Push in on the outside edges of both sections of clay. The clay along the "fault" will buckle and slide. Earthquake!

THAR SHE BLOWS!

26

There's no need to run for cover from this safe model of a real erupting volcano.

What You'll Need: Tall jar with lid; water; baking soda; dishwashing liquid; red or orange food coloring; large plastic container or wash basin; dirt or plaster of Paris and paints; pine cones (optional); vinegar

When a real volcano erupts, you don't want to be there. After all, the lava that spews out of a volcano is rock that is so hot it has become liquid. But you can get an idea what it's like by making your own volcano.

First, get a tall, thin jar. The kind of jar that pickles or olives come in works well. In the jar, mix together ¼ cup water, ¼ cup baking soda, three tablespoons dishwashing liquid, and a few drops of red or orange food coloring. Put the lid on the jar. Set the jar in the center of a big container. Next, build a "mountain" of dirt or sand around the jar. (It will work better if the dirt or sand is slightly wet.) If you'd like, you can cover the mountain with plaster of Paris, and paint it to look like a real volcano. You can even decorate it with pine cones to look like trees.

Now... it's lava time! Take the lid off the jar, quickly pour in ¼ cup of vinegar, and stand back. Watch your volcano erupt.

SLEEPING GIANTS

Just because a volcano has been asleep for a long time does not mean that it is no longer a threat. One volcano that was asleep, called Mount St. Helens in the state of Washington, hadn't erupted since 1857. But, in 1980, it erupted violently, causing it to become more than 1,000 feet shorter than it had been.

'TITES OR 'MITES?

27

If you sat in a cave for thousands of years, you could watch stalactites and stalagmites form. Or you could make your own in a matter of days.

What You'll Need: Two jars, water, Epsom salts, string, small weights, plate

Fill two jars with warm water. Mix in Epsom salts until no more will dissolve. Wet the string and tie a weight to each end. Drop one end of the string into each jar. Put a plate between the two jars, with the string hanging over the plate.

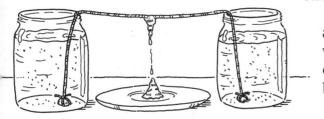

Check your "cave" at least once a day to see if stalactites and stalagmites have formed. By the way, if you're wondering which are 'tites and which are 'mites: Stala*ctites* have to hold on *tight* to stay on the ceiling of the cave. Stalag*mites* have to be *mighty* to stand up on the floor of the cave.

NATURE'S DISGUISES

28

There's more to the world than meets the eye when you try some of these experiments with camouflage.

Nature is an expert at camouflage, a word that means to disguise, or to hide. Here are just a few examples: Polar bears blend in with the ice and snow of their Arctic habitat. If they didn't, they wouldn't be able to sneak up on the prey they need to survive. Ermine and some kinds of weasels have an even more interesting way of camouflaging themselves. In summer, they are brown to blend in with the woods where they live. But ermine and weasels that live in the north turn white in winter, when they are surrounded by snow. This makes it hard for predators, such as coyotes and wolves, to see them. The insects that we call walking sticks look like just that: sticks. They look so much like sticks that you can't tell they're insects unless you see them move.

Take a walk around your neighborhood and see if you can find examples of camouflage. Then, try to imitate nature by camouflaging yourself. How could you dress to camouflage yourself in winter, spring, summer, and fall? Play hide and seek with a friend—see how well you can camouflage yourselves.

29 WHERE'S THE NORTH POLE?

What direction are you facing right now? You'll know the answer when you make this handy homemade compass

What You'll Need: Pie pan, water, dishwashing liquid, magnet, needle, ¼-inch slice of cork

Fill a pie pan with water. Add a small amount of dishwashing liquid. Now you'll need to magnetize a needle. To do this, use a bar magnet with the north end marked. Scrape the needle across the north end of the magnet, from the eye of the needle to its point. Do this about 15 times. It's important to scrape the needle in the same direction every time—don't rub it back and forth on the magnet.

Carefully poke the needle through a small piece of cork. Float the cork in the middle of the pie pan. Like magic, the needle will always point north. If you walked far enough in that direction, you'd find yourself at the North Pole! That's because the Earth is like a giant magnet, with one end in the North Pole and the other end in South Pole.

THE FLAT EARTH

About 2,300 years ago, a Greek scientist named Aristotle decided that the Earth was round, not flat like other people believed. Most people laughed at Aristotle, and it wasn't until Columbus traveled to America in the late 1400s that others started to take Aristotle's theory seriously. There is still an organization called The Flat Earth Society, and its members believe that Aristotle made a mistake.

COLOR YOUR WORLD

30

This fun matching game will help you find out what colors Mother Nature likes best.

What You'll Need: Squares of paper in various bright and dull colors, scissors

Collect paper in as many different colors as you can find. Look through cupboards, old colored paper supplies, and any place paper is stored to find old pieces of gray cardboard, faded construction paper, and other dull colors. Collect brighter colors as well, including vivid neon colors. Cut the paper into 2-inch squares.

Give each of the players five squares picked at random and take them outdoors. Tell them they must find something in nature that matches each of the squares exactly. For instance, a square of green paper may not be the same shade of green as grass. The player must keep looking at leaves, moss, and other plants to find an exact match. See if you can figure out what colors are used most in nature.

You can also let the players pick the colors they want to find. Many people like to pick the neon colors rather than the dull colors, but they soon learn the dull colors are much easier to match, while the neon colors are nearly impossible!

31

WHAT IS IT?

You'll have to use all your other senses when you play this nature version of Blindman's Buff.

What You'll Need: Strip of cloth to use as a blindfold

This is a nature game to play with a partner. Have your partner blindfold you and guide you around to touch, smell, and listen to different things in nature. Can you guess what each thing is? Do you notice how things feel, smell, and sound more than you have before? Even familiar places can seem like strange new worlds! Trade places with your partner, letting him or her wear the blindfold while you are the guide.

TRAIL SIGNS

32

Early pioneers and explorers marked their way for others to follow. See if you can do the same thing.

What You'll Need: Nature objects

Whenever people have moved through new territory they marked the trail so they would not get lost. Native Americans often bent trees to the ground to mark trails. Some of these "trail trees" have grown to full-sized trees. Early explorers and scouts used axe marks on trees. Outdoor youth clubs of today use temporary signs of twigs, grass, and stones, borrowed from the Native Americans.

I went this way.

To play a trail marking game, have one person lay a cross-country trail through woods or an open field. The person should make trail markers twenty or so paces apart. (Be careful not to harm any live plants when you are making your markers.) Arrow shapes, stacks of rocks, or bundles of grass all say "I went this way." A bend in the grass bundle, or a rock beside the pile means "turn this way." Three of anything means "warning." And X means "do not go this way." A circle means "this is the end of the trail." You can use the pictures on this page to help or come up with some of your own. The rest of the players try to follow the trail and see where the person ended up.

Turn this way.

Don't go this way.

WHAT'S A WHIFFLEPOOF?

33

Try playing this game, used to teach tracking skills, with your friends.

What You'll Need: Small log (about 4 inches in diameter, 18 inches long), a few dozen large nails, screw eye, heavy twine.

To make the Whifflepoof: With the help of a parent or adult, take a small log and drive a few dozen nails into it, leaving about two inches of each nail still sticking out, until the log bristles with nails. Take a large screw eye and screw it into one end of the log. Tie a length of rope about four feet long to the screw eye.

To play the game: Have one person drag the Whifflepoof through woods or an open field while the other players close their eyes. The person dragging the Whifflepoof should make as long a trail as possible in the area. When the trail is done, the rest of the players attempt to follow it.

HAPPY TRAILS

34

Turn your backyard, local park, or camp into a nature trail.

What You'll Need: Stakes and small thin boards to make signs, paint

If you have a favorite natural area, make a trail to point out its interesting features. You can make a permanent trail on private land, or a temporary one in a park for a special occasion. Be sure to ask adults for permission.

Make small signs from scrap wood. Paint them, and use paint or permanent markers to write out descriptions of the interesting features or things to do at each station. Nail the signs to stakes. Here are some ideas for stations:

• Give the name of a tree and list some interesting facts about it.

• Point out a tree that has a bird nest in it. Tell what kind of bird has made the nest.

• State that an animal has made its home near the station. Challenge your readers to find it.

• Have the reader stop and listen for the call of a particular bird that lives near the station.

• Put a station near some sweet-scented flower or other plant.

PAINT BOX

35

Who needs to buy paints and markers when nature has a free supply of coloring tools for you?

What You'll Need: Leaves, bark, flowers, rocks, soil, sticks, berries from the lawn or garden, white paper, fine sandpaper

The colors you see in flowers, leaves, and berries are from chemicals called pigments. Pigments also give color to paints, markers, and crayons. You can use natural pigments to create colorful pictures. Find a variety of flowers, leaves, and berries outdoors. Rub them on the paper to make marks. Experiment to see what kinds of colors you can make, then make a picture with them. Try bark, dirt, sticks, or rocks to see if they will make marks as well.

After you have experimented on white paper and learned to make pictures, try making pictures on fine sandpaper. The colors will come out more strongly, and you will have an attractive picture to frame and put on your wall.

NATURE'S ORCHESTRA

36

You and your friends can strike up the band with these musical instruments made from natural materials.

What You'll Need: Nature objects, cans

Remember: Don't harm live plants or disturb animals in their habitats during this project.

With a group of friends, collect rocks, gravel, sand, sticks, shells, and anything else from nature that you can use to make musical instruments. Use your imagination! Put rocks in cans to shake. Use sticks as drumsticks. Maybe you can make a drum from a hollow log or from bark. See if you and your friends can make beautiful music together.

NATURE SCAVENGER HUNT

37

As you explore nature, be careful not to disturb any plants or animals.

What You'll Need: Paper, pen, nature objects

Make a list of things you might find in nature in your neighborhood. They should all be things that nature "casts off," such as dropped leaves and seed pods, feathers, small stones, etc. That way, you won't be taking things that nature still needs! Make a copy of the list for each person who wants to join the scavenger hunt. Then set off, alone or in pairs, to find everything on the list. You can even have a race to see who finds the objects first!

Another way to have a nature scavenger hunt is to find things in nature but not touch them or bring them home. When you play this way, you just mark off each thing on your list as you find it.

This activity is a good way to collect the natural objects you'll need for other activities in the book. For example, you could look for pine cones to make pine cone creatures, feathers to make quill pens, interesting leaves for leaf stencils, shells for shell art, etc.

38

B-I-N-G-O!

Try this special kind of bingo that you play in nature.

What You'll Need: Ruler, paper, pen, crayons or markers

First, make your bingo cards. Use a ruler to make a grid of 16 squares on a piece of paper. (Draw three lines across, and three lines up and down.) In each square, write the name or draw the picture of something in nature: a bird, insect, animal, tree, flower, etc. They should all be things that can be found in your neighborhood. You'll need to make several cards, and make sure each card has a different arrangement and at least some different nature objects compared to other cards.

When you're ready to play, get a group of friends and give a bingo card to each person. Go on a nature walk. When a player sees something that is on his or her card, the person marks off that square. The first person to mark all the squares in a row wins. Or, you can play super nature bingo: The first person to mark all the squares on a card wins.

WHAT'S THAT SMELL?

39

Find out how dogs and cats feel when sniffing their way around a park.

What You'll Need: Spray bottle, strong-smelling flavoring extract (vanilla, mint, lemon), water.

Humans have an amazing ability to distinguish hundreds of different scents, but our sense of smell isn't nearly as well-developed as it is in many other mammals. This game will let you "perceive" the world as many animals do—by scent.

Fill a spray bottle with water and add one or two teaspoons of a strong-scented extract. (Peppermint, lemon, and vanilla work well.) Make a trial spray on a tree to see if the scent is strong enough to detect. Then have the players close their eyes while one person runs ahead through a wooded area with the spray bottle. The person laying the trail should spray trees and other objects along the way. If playing in grassy fields, be careful not to leave an obvious track through the grass. When the trail maker is done, the rest of the players try to follow the trail.

MICRO-HIKE

40

You may not get far, but you'll see plenty of things right under your nose!

What You'll Need: Magnifying glasses

This may be the shortest hike you've ever been on, but it's bound to be one of the most interesting. Find an area in woods or a grassy field where there are fallen logs, rocks, or other places where small creatures can hide. Look for areas that have a lot of variation in a short space.

Everyone on the hike should have a magnifying glass. Now get down on your hands and knees. Move *very slowly* through the area you've chosen, peering through your magnifying glass as though you were looking through the porthole of a spaceship. Look closely at the moss on a fallen log. You might spot tiny mushrooms and molds. Gently lift loose bark to see if any insects or other animals have made their homes there. (Be sure to put the bark back.) Do the same for rocks or other objects. Search among the fallen leaves or right at the base of tall grasses. You'll be amazed at the abundance of life you find!

OUR FAVORITE PLANET

41

Considering that the Earth is where you live, you probably don't give it much thought. You'll be surprised when you read about our amazing home.

What You'll Need: One or more books about the Earth, paper, pen

Our planet is a pretty interesting place. Scientists think the Earth is about 4,600,000,000 years old. (That's more than four and a half billion years.) It's 93,000,000 miles from the sun. (That's 93 million miles.) And at the center of the Earth, the temperature is about 9,000 degrees. (That's very hot!)

Check out some books about the Earth from your library, and see what else you can learn about your home. Write a report telling the most interesting things you learned from the books you read. Or try to find 10 fun facts to share with your friends. You can also invent an "Earth quiz" to test their knowledge of this amazing planet.

ARMORED MUDBALLS

Mud has a reputation of being just plain boring. In a few places around the world, however, there are actually armored mudballs, fossilized circles of mud formed about 200 million years ago. These armored mudballs are about the size of a baseball, reddish brown in color, with little pebbles poking out. They were created when pieces of mud fell out of an ancient stream into nearby beds of stone.

HOW'S THE WEATHER?

It's an age-old question: What kind of weather will we have and how can we know? Some may laugh at the weather forecasters, but weather is tough to predict. So many things may change it! In this chapter you'll learn about wind, rain, snow, and many other things you see everyday. As you learn, you'll notice sunlight, wind, and water all affect the weather.

42 — CHIME IN

Gather shells, small stones, or other items from nature that you think would make a nice-sounding wind chime.

What You'll Need: Nature items, nylon fishing line or dental floss, stick, nail or drill, jewelry fittings and glue (optional)

Use nylon fishing line or dental floss to hang each of your items from a stick. There are several ways to prepare your items for hanging. You can use a nail or drill to make a small hole in each item. Or, go to a crafts store and buy some jewelry fittings. These are small metal pieces with rings. Glue a fitting to each item, and thread the line through the ring on the fitting. Be sure to hang the items at about the same length, so they'll touch one another when the wind blows them. Use more line to tie the stick where the wind will "tickle" the chimes. Try hanging your chimes in different places to see where the wind blows gently or with more force.

CLOCK THE WIND

43

How fast is the wind blowing today? Make a wind-speed gauge that will tell you.

What You'll Need: Two hollow balls (rubber balls, tennis balls, or ping-pong balls), nails, two sticks of the same length, one-foot wooden 2×4, drill, wooden board for a base, wax or oil

Ask an adult to help you with this project. First, take two small, hollow balls and cut them in half. Nail the ball halves to the ends of two sticks with the cut sides facing outward as shown in the illustration. Paint one half ball a different color from the other three. Next, nail the two sticks together at right angles so they form an X. Make sure you join the two sticks at their exact centers, so the joined sticks will balance on the nail. Use a long nail so that the end of the nail comes through both sticks.

Now make the base. Have an adult drill a hole in the end of a one-foot length of a wooden 2×4. The hole should be a bit larger than the nail that holds the two sticks together. Attach the 2×4 to a wooden base, and set the nail in the drilled hole. (Put a little wax or oil in the hole so the gauge will turn easily.)

Now, put your wind-speed gauge in the wind. Count the number of times it turns around in 30 seconds. (Count by the painted half ball.) Write that number down and divide it by five. The answer is the wind speed in miles per hour.

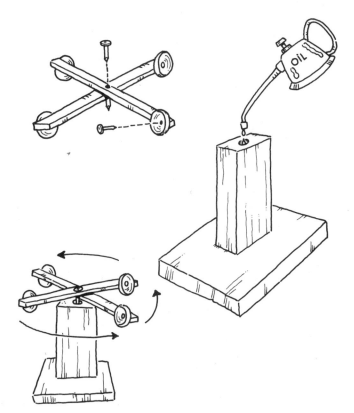

WHAT KIND OF WIND?

44

Be a wind detective! There are clues all around you that help tell how fast the wind is blowing.

In the early 1800s, a British admiral named Francis Beaufort came up with a system so that sailors had a way to describe the wind's strength that meant the same thing to everybody. The table below shows the Beaufort Scale, which shows how each level of wind looks both at sea and on land. Each day, look for clues to how strong the wind is. Is it a 0 day or a 7 day? Is it a light breeze or a fresh breeze?

The Beaufort Scale:

Type of wind	Clues at sea	Clues on land
0 Calm	Smooth water	Smoke rises straight up
1 Light air	Small ripples	Smoke drifts sideways
2 Light breeze	Small wavelets	Leaves and weather vanes move
3 Gentle breeze	Larger wavelets; foam	Twigs move
4 Moderate breeze	Small waves	Branches move; flags flap
5 Fresh breeze	Medium waves; spray	Small trees sway
6 Strong breeze	Large waves, up to ten feet	Large branches sway
7 Strong wind	Waves 18 - 24 feet	Larger trees sway; flags stand straight out
8 Fresh gale	Waves up to 23 - 30 feet	Twigs break; hard to walk
9 Strong gale	Waves 25 - 33 feet	Signs blow down
10 Storm	Waves 29 - 40 feet	Trees fall over
11 Violent storm	Waves 37 - 50 feet, foam covers surface	Widespread damage
12 Hurricane	Waves 45 - 60 feet, heavy spray and foam	Widespread destruction

BLOWING IN THE WIND

45

The wind is sometimes like a bus or train. It picks up passengers from one place and transports them to another.

What You'll Need: Cardboard, string, vegetable oil or petroleum jelly

Get a piece of cardboard that is the size of a piece of notebook paper or larger. Make a small hole on one end of the cardboard, and tie a piece of string through the hole. Smear one side of the cardboard with vegetable oil or petroleum jelly. On a windy day, hang the cardboard from a tree using the string. Make sure the oily side of the cardboard is facing the wind. Leave the cardboard in the wind for an hour or more. Then go back and see what the wind has carried onto the cardboard. You may find seeds, insects, pollen, dust, or other tidbits of nature.

Some plants (like the dandelion) use wind to help scatter their seeds far away. Sometimes the seeds can be carried for several miles or more! Small spiders can hang by their thread and let the wind blow them from spot to spot. What other ways can you think of to use wind?

TRADE WINDS

Have you ever heard the expression "trade winds?" If so, have you wondered where it came from? Well, wonder no more. Long ago, people delivered things that were for sale by ship. Buying and selling items was also known as "trade." Sailors knew about the steady bands of wind that blow all around the world, just above and below the equator. They called these winds the trade winds and used them to travel the world.

TWISTER IN A BOTTLE

46

Most real tornadoes are made of air, but you can demonstrate how tornadoes work using water.

What You'll Need: Water, two 2-liter bottles, cardboard, knife, tape

Pour water into a 2-liter plastic bottle until it is about ¾ full. Cut a circle of cardboard as big around as the bottle's opening. Then cut a ¼-inch hole in the center. Place the cardboard circle on top of your water bottle's opening. Turn another 2-liter bottle upside down and tape the two bottles together, top to top. Wrap the bottle necks with tape, so the connection doesn't leak. Now turn the bottles upside down, so the full bottle is on top. With one hand, hold the bottom bottle to steady it. With the other hand, begin moving the top bottle in a circle. Watch what happens: a tornado in a bottle.

Water tornadoes, such as the one you just made, happen in nature, too. When a tornado forms over water, it's called a waterspout.

STUCK ON TORNADOES

While people worry about the damage a tornado may cause to their property, a tornado in Illinois in the year 1883 caused an unexpected clean-up job for one family. They had hurried to the cellar, where they all ended up covered with something quite sticky. *Popular Science Monthly* guessed that they had gotten covered with sap from trees and juice from leaves, carried by the strong tornado winds.

WIND SOCK

47

Socks do more than keep your toes warm. A wind sock can tell you which way the wind is blowing—and how fast, too!

What You'll Need: Yardstick, light cloth such as muslin (one yard will make a large sock), scissors, needle and thread, wire, fishing line, thin wood, stake or old broom handle, large nail

With help from a parent or adult, use a yardstick to help you cut one square yard of light fabric. Fold it in half diagonally. Mark the center of one of the narrow edges. Cut from the mark to the corner at the other end. You will have two long triangles of fabric. Cut two inches off of the pointed end. Sew the long edges together to make a cone. (An adult may be able to help you sew with a sewing machine.) Shape light stiff wire into a hoop large enough to keep the large end of the cone open. Fold the edges of the fabric around the wire and sew in place. Cut four pieces of heavy fishing line, about two feet long. Poke four small holes through the fabric around the hoop at even distances. Tie a piece of fishing line through each. Cut a square of wood and paint letters for each of the four directions on the corners. Glue the square to the top of the stake or old broom handle. Drive a nail through the center of the square. Tie the lines of your wind sock to the nail.

Hang your wind sock outside your home, making sure the letters are facing the correct direction, and observe the angles of the windsock on different days. Note which angles go with what weather conditions. Make a chart of your information and use the chart to help you estimate wind speed.

WEATHER VANE

Which way is the wind blowing? With a little work you'll have your own weather vane to tell you.

What You'll Need: 18-inch strip of wood (about ¼ inch thick and ½ inch wide), sandpaper, drill, flat piece of very thin wood (about four inches long and three inches wide), thin wire nails, hot glue gun and glue sticks, small fishing weights, spray paint, four-inch square of thin wood, small metal nut, one fourpenny nail, stake, compass

With adult help, sand the wood strip smooth. Lay it flat and drill a small hole eight inches from one end (big enough for the fourpenny nail to go through). Next, cut a fin from thin wood. It should be four inches long, three inches wide at one end, and one inch wide at the other. Now turn your thin stick so the narrow side faces up. Lay the fin on the narrow side on the end of the stick that is eight inches from the hole. Carefully nail it in place with thin wire nails. Run the fourpenny nail through the hole in the stick. See if the vane balances. If it does not, hot glue small fishing weights opposite the fin. Paint with spray paint. Cut a four-inch square of thin wood and spray paint it. When dry, paint on the letters of the four directions on each of the sides. Paint the stake. When it is dry, glue the painted square of wood to the top. Lay a small nut on the center of the square, then the pointer. Nail the fourpenny nail through the hole in the pointer so that it goes through the nut, the center of the square, and into the stake. Set the weather vane out in an open area. Use a compass to align it. When reading the weather vane, remember that it will point into the wind, showing where the wind is coming from.

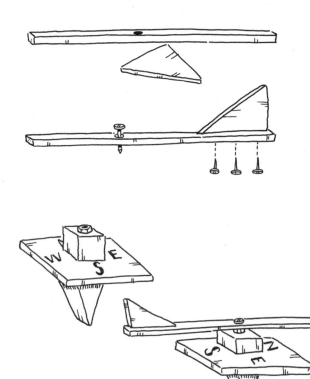

SNOWMAN COOKIES

49

These treats are great for a cold, snowy day. Or bring a little winter to your kitchen in the summer.

What You'll Need: 1 package (20 ounces) refrigerated chocolate chip cookie dough, cookie sheet, 1½ cups sifted powered sugar, 2 tablespoons milk, decorations: candy corn, gumdrops, chocolate chips, licorice, and other assorted small candies

Ask an adult to help you make these snowman cookies. Preheat your oven to 375°F. Remove dough from wrapper according to package directions. Cut dough into 12 equal sections. Divide each section into 3 balls: small, medium, and large. For each snowman, place the three balls in a row, ¼-inch apart, on an ungreased cookie sheet. Repeat with remaining dough. Allow space between each snowman, so they have room to spread while baking.

Bake 10 to 12 minutes or until edges are very lightly browned. Cool 4 minutes on cookie sheets. Remove whole snowmen to wire racks; cool completely.

Mix powdered sugar and milk in medium bowl until smooth. This mixture is your snow! Pour over cookies. Let cookies stand for 20 minutes or until set.

Using assorted candies, create faces, hats, arms, and anything else you can think of to decorate your snow people. Makes 12 cookies.

CLOUDY CONDITIONS

50

Whether it's a rainy or sunny day, bring a part of the sky inside. Make a cloud in a bottle.

What You'll Need: Empty soda bottle, candle, matches

With help from an adult, hold a narrow-mouthed bottle over a candle flame for a few seconds. Then blow out the candle. Wipe the rim of the bottle and quickly blow into it. The warm moisture in your breath will condense and turn into a "cloud" in the bottle.

RAIN GAUGE

51

Next time it rains, keep track of just how wet it is out there with your own working rain gauge.

What You'll Need: Piece of thin wood (about eight inches long and four inches wide), sandpaper, spray paint (optional), old test tube or olive jar, modeling clay (optional), wire, drill, 6-inch plastic ruler, acrylic paint, stake, paper, pen

With help from a parent or other adult, sand the piece of wood smooth. If you wish you can paint it with spray paint. If you are using an old test tube, press a small amount of modeling clay in the bottom to make it level. Next, lay your test tube or olive jar on the board and mark the board so that the top of the jar or tube extends about an inch beyond the top edge of the board. Mark the board on both sides of the tube near the top and near the bottom. Have an adult drill small holes where you made marks. Wire the tube or olive jar to the board by running wire through the small holes and around the tube. Twist tightly in the back.

Use a ruler to help you paint marks on the side of the tube. Start from the bottom and paint heavy lines every inch. Then paint thin lines to mark quarter inches. Fasten your rain gauge to a stake. Be sure to put it someplace where overhanging trees or large buildings won't block the rain. After a rain, check the tube to see how much rain fell. Then empty the gauge, and return it to the stake. Keep track of your readings on a chart.

SAVE IT FOR A SUNNY DAY

It's hard to sit indoors all day, watching the rain fall from your seat at the window. Maybe you'd planned to play baseball that day, or maybe your family was going to have a picnic, but the festivities got rained out. But look on the bright side. There are places on Earth where it rains almost every single day! Those places are called tropical rainforests, and they get between 100 and 400 inches of rain every single year.

WHEN IT RAINS, IT POURS

52

Who says you can't make it rain indoors? No need to wait for a rainy day—just make some rain yourself!

What You'll Need: Pot, water, glass jar with lid, towel, ice

Ask an adult to bring a pot of water to a boil; let it cool slightly. Pour the water into a jar, and put on the lid. Place the jar on a towel. Then put ice on the jar's lid. Watch a rainstorm begin in the jar as hot water condenses on the lid and rains down into the water.

Watching your 'rainstorm' makes it easy to imagine what happens when a cold front (a mass of cold air) comes into contact with warm air: Moisture from the warm air is pushed up, clouds are formed, and soon it's raining.

53

LET IT RAIN

Drip, drip, drop! Use raindrops to create beautiful and unique paintings you can frame and hang on a wall.

What You'll Need: Water-soluble paint or markers, posterboard

Use water-soluble paint or markers to make solid blocks of color on posterboard. Then put the paper in the rain for a short time. Watch as the rain "paints" your paper. Take the paper out of the rain when you think the painting is finished (before all the color is washed away). Experiment by making raindrop paintings in a light rain or drizzle, a steady rain, and a real downpour.

NATURAL MATH

54

You don't have to be a weather forecaster to calculate how far away lightning is. Just take a look.

What You'll Need: Stopwatch or watch with a second hand.

Where there is lightning, there is thunder. Since light travels faster than speed, you see the flash before you hear the sound. You can use the thunder to figure out how far away the lightning is. Watch for a flash of lightning. When you see it, use a stopwatch or second hand to count the seconds between the flash and the thunder that follows it. Write down the number of seconds, and divide that number by five. The answer tells you how far away from you the lightning was in miles. Did you know that not all lightning bolts touch the earth. In fact, two-thirds of all lightning occurs between clouds or within the same cloud. But that doesn't mean it's safe to go out in a thunderstorm! During a storm, avoid tall objects (like trees) and don't touch anything metal. You should also stay away from electrical appliances, telephones, and water until the storm is over.

"WHAT WAS THAT?"

55

Make up your own legend to explain thunder and lightning—or any other weather phenomenon.

In ancient times, people had no way to know what thunder and lightning were or what caused them. So they made up stories to "explain" these mysteries. One Native American tribe believed that thunder and lightning were the signs of gods attacking evil men on Earth. In fact, most ancient people thought thunder was the sound of gods either talking or fighting, and lightning flashes were their spears.

Imagine that you lived long before modern science. Make up a legend of your own to explain thunder and lightning. Write your legend, and draw pictures to illustrate it.

MAKE A HYGROMETER

56

Sometimes people say, "It's not the heat, it's the humidity," to explain why hot weather bothers them. Use this instrument to find out just how humid it is outside.

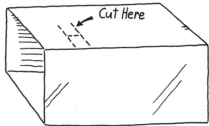

What You'll Need: One hair at least nine inches long, half-gallon cardboard milk carton, scissors, darning needle, broom straw, glue, paper clip, tape, penny, plain index card

Wash the hair clean with soap and water. Under adult supervision, cut a small "H" in the side of the carton as shown, about one half the length of the darning needle. Bend back the tabs and push the needle through. Poke a broom straw into the eye of the needle and glue in place. At the end of the carton, cut a small slit and push the paper clip through it. Glue in place. Tape one end of the hair to the paper clip. Lay the hair over the needle, loop it around the needle once, then let it hang over the end of the box opposite the paper clip. Tape the penny to the free end of the hair. Draw a half-circle on the index card and divide the half-circle with ten marks. Label them one through ten beginning on the left side. Glue the index card to the box under the broom straw. Take your completed hygrometer into the bathroom and run hot water in the shower until the mirror fogs up. The air is 100 percent humid and will cause the hair to stretch. Adjust the straw so it points to 10. Put the hygrometer outdoors in a sheltered place, such as under a porch. Tap it gently a few times before taking a reading, to make sure the straw isn't stuck in place.

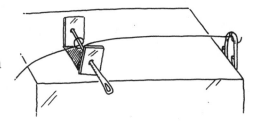

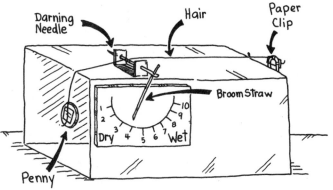

FEELING PRESSURED?

57

You may not feel it, but the air around you has pressure. This simple experiment will help demonstrate its invisible force.

What You'll Need: Cup, index card

Fill a cup all the way to the top with water. Place an index card over the top of the cup. Hold the card in place, and turn the cup upside down. Slowly, carefully, let go of the index card. It should stay in place, held by the pressure of the air beneath it. Be sure to work over a sink in case your cup slips and the water spills.

FOGGY NOTIONS

58

Did you ever wonder what exactly fog is? This project will help clear up the mystery.

What You'll Need: Bottle, hot water, rubbing alcohol, ice cube

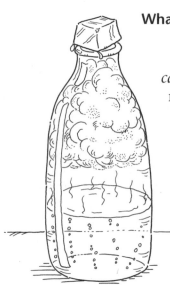

You've probably seen fog. That's because when fog is around, it's about all you *can* see. Well, fog is a cloud that forms very close to the ground. In nature, when a mass of cold air bumps into a mass of warm humid air, millions of tiny droplets of water are formed. That's fog. Here's a way to get some cold air and some warm air together and make fog:

Fill a bottle ⅓ full of very hot water. Add a few drops of rubbing alcohol. Put a piece of ice over the top of the bottle and watch fog develop.

SO MUCH PRESSURE!

59

You can make a water barometer that will show you the changes in the air pressure.

What You'll Need: Ruler, modeling clay, water, bowl, clear plastic bottle, string, paper, pen or pencil

First, stick a ruler into a lump of modeling clay. Then put the clay and ruler in the bottom of a bowl. (The ruler should be standing up straight.) Put about three inches of water into the bowl.

Next get a narrow, clear plastic bottle. Fill it about ¾ full of water. Cover the top of the bottle with your hand, turn it upside down, and put it into the bowl next to the ruler. Once the bottle top is underwater, you can take your hand away. With the bottle still standing upside down, tie the ruler to the bottle with string.

Cut a strip of paper about four inches long. Make a scale on it by making a mark every ¼ inch. Halfway down the strip, make a longer line to show the halfway mark. Tape this strip of paper to the bottle with the halfway mark at the same level as the water in the bottle.

Now you have a water barometer. The water in the bottle will move up and down as the air pressure changes. As the air pressure in the room increases, it will push down on the water in the bowl, forcing water up into the bottle. Then you can see yourself that the air pressure is high. If the air pressure is low, the bowl's water will rise, the bottle's water will sink, and you'll get a lower pressure reading.

HOT, HOT, HOT!

A Chinook is a hot and dry wind. In 1943, people in Rapid City, South Dakota, felt a Chinook raise their temperature from 10 to 55 degrees in just 15 minutes!

THE WIND-CHILL FACTOR

60

Cold weather feels even colder when it's windy. Professional weather forecasters call this the "wind-chill factor."

What You'll Need: Thermometer, wind-speed gauge (see page 35)

Your body is normally surrounded by a thin layer of warm air, and it protects you. The wind, however, actually blows away that layer of warm air. So, you feel much colder on windy days. Using a thermometer, measure the temperature. Then calculate the speed of the wind with the wind-speed gauge. Combine the numbers on the chart below to determine the wind-chill factor. Use the wind-chill factor to help you dress for the weather. Bundle up for how cold it *feels*, not how cold it is!

Find the place on the chart where the wind speed and the temperature meet. That's the wind-chill factor. Example: If the wind speed is 10 mph and the temperature is 25 degrees, the wind-chill factor is 10 degrees.

Wind Speed, miles per hour	Temperature, Fahrenheit						
0	30	25	20	15	10	5	0
5	27	22	16	11	6	0	-5
10	16	10	3	-3	-9	-15	-22
15	9	2	-5	-11	-18	-25	-31
20	4	-3	-10	-17	-24	-31	-39
25	1	-7	-15	-22	-29	-36	-44
30	-2	-11	-18	-27	-33	-43	-49

WINTER'S DIAMONDS

61

If you want to make icicles, don't forget the most important ingredient: a cold winter night.

What You'll Need: Pencil, plastic cup, string, water, needle or pin

Using a sharp pencil, poke three or four holes around the lip of a plastic cup. Tie several inches of string through each hole, then tie the ends of the strings together to make a hanger for the cup. Use a needle or pin to poke a very small hole in the bottom of the cup. Be careful not to poke yourself. Fill the cup with water. The water should drip very slowly out the hole in the bottom. On a cold night, before you go to bed, hang the cup outside on a branch or nail. Overnight, an icicle will form at the bottom of the cup.

THIS WILL CRACK YOU UP

62

It's true, winter can be hard on everybody—even on rocks. See how the cold affects more than just your toes.

What You'll Need: Egg, small sealable plastic bag

Put an egg in a sealed plastic bag and put the bag in the freezer overnight. In the morning, see what the freezing temperature did to the egg. When the egg freezes, it expands and breaks its shell. Winter freezes do the same thing to rocks that have moisture in them. The moisture expands as it freezes, causing the rocks to break. When you're out walking in the winter, see if you can find rocks that have been in nature's deep freeze. A rock that is broken into pieces but still lying in its original shape is probably a victim of winter's icy strength.

BE A CUT-UP

63

Nature's snowflakes are beautiful, but they don't last long. You can make long-lasting snowflakes out of construction paper.

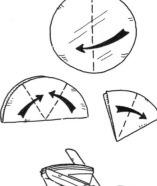

What You'll Need: Paper, plate, scissors

Trace around a plate to make a circle on a piece of paper. (All nature's snowflakes are white, of course, but yours can be any color you like.) Cut out the circle.

Fold the circle in half. Then fold it in thirds. Fold it in half one more time.

Use a scissors to cut small pieces out of the paper. Then unfold the circle to see what your snowflake looks like. Because of the way snow crystals form, every snowflake has six rays—just like your paper snowflakes.

WARM, FUZZY SNOW

64

You can use cotton balls to create a 3-D winter scene that won't melt in the spring.

What You'll Need: Paint, paintbrush, shoe box, cotton balls, glue, crayons, glitter (optional)

Paint the inside of a shoe box. Use a good sky-colored paint like blue or gray. When the paint is dry, tilt the shoe box on its side, so the narrow part is faced down. Then make a snow scene using cotton balls for the snow. Use your imagination to make snow-covered hills and trees, snow people, snow animals, and more. (If you want to, you can make your drawing in crayon first, then glue on the cotton.) Add glitter to make your snow sparkle like the real thing!

SNOW ICE CREAM

65

Long ago people figured out the easiest way to make ice cream is to use snow.

What You'll Need: Clean snow, bowl, sugar, vanilla extract, milk or cream

Scoop some freshly fallen snow into a big, chilled bowl. (Make sure the snow you take is clean and white. If the snow is brown or yellow, it will taste yucky.) Nestle the bowl in the snow to keep it cold while you make snow ice cream. Add a little sugar, a few drops of vanilla extract, and some very cold milk or cream. Stir together and eat. You might like to take your tasty treat inside to enjoy by a warm fire. Experiment with different flavors of snow ice cream. Try adding some cinnamon or cocoa powder.

AS WARM AS...SNOW?

66

We all know snow is cold, but can it help keep you warm? Take a snowbank's temperature.

What You'll Need: Two thermometers, snow, stick or branch

For this activity, you'll need to wait for a day when it's very cold (at least 10 degrees Fahrenheit or lower). Be sure to dress warmly! Find a large snowbank and dig a small hole deep into its base. Put a thermometer in the hole. Now put a second thermometer outside the snowbank but also outside of the rays of the sun. Put a stick or branch nearby to mark the spot. Leave both thermometers overnight.

The next day, compare the two thermometers. Is there a difference in the temperatures outside and inside the snowbank? The colder it gets outside, the bigger the difference you'll find between the two temperatures. This is because snow has the ability to insulate and protect things from even colder weather. And that's why when it gets really cold, small animals will tunnel into the snow to shelter themselves from the deep chill.

67

MY, WHAT BIG FEET YOU HAVE

Snowshoes allow people to walk on top of deep snow, instead of sinking into it. Make your own shoe box snowshoes.

What You'll Need: Two shoe boxes or a few fallen evergreen boughs, large rubber bands or old shoelaces

Snowshoes work by spreading a person's weight over a larger area of snow, so the snow can support the weight. Here are a couple of quick and easy ways to make snowshoes:

Use big rubber bands or shoelaces to strap shoe boxes or evergreen boughs to the bottoms of your boots. Now try walking in the snow. You'll find that walking in snowshoes is like walking in swim fins: It's important to lift the front of your foot high with each step.

UPS AND DOWNS

68

Here's how you can keep track of temperature changes, just like weather forecasters do.

What You'll Need: Thermometer, paper, pen

Put a thermometer outdoors—out of the sun—and check it at the same time each day. Record the daily temperatures. Make a graph of your temperature readings like the one in the picture. Every week or so, connect the dots on the graph to make a line showing the temperature ups and downs. Which day was coldest? Which was warmest? What trend do you see over time? Is it getting colder or warmer?

EXAMINE SNOWFLAKES

69

You've heard that no two snowflakes are alike, right? Take a look and see if it's true.

What You'll Need: Black construction paper, magnifying glass

Do this activity on a snowy day. Put a piece of black construction paper outside where it's cold, but not where it will get snowed on. Let the paper chill for several minutes.

Then catch snowflakes on the paper and look at them under a magnifying glass. Are they really all different from one another? In what ways are they all alike? Scientists have found that snowflakes come in seven basic geometric shapes. However, snowflakes have in-finite different—and beautiful—varieties within those categories.

When you go inside, you might want to draw snowflakes as they looked under the magnifying glass.

SNOWFLAKE FACT

Snowflakes are actually six-sided ice crystals, ones that are created in clouds when the temperature is below freezing. In order for you to have good snow for snowmen and snowball fights, the air has to stay cold as the snowflakes fall. Otherwise the ice crystals will melt. But, if the air is too cold throughout the snowflake's descent, the snow will not stick together well enough for snowballs.

JUST HOW HOT IS IT?

Most thermometers are made with mercury, a poisonous metal. But you can make a safe thermometer using water.

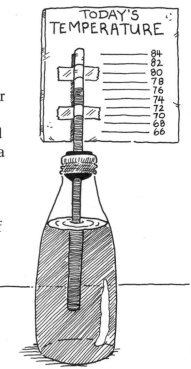

What You'll Need: Soft drink bottle, water, food coloring, clear drinking straw, modeling clay, index card, tape, pen or pencil

Fill a small soft drink bottle almost full of water (about ⅘ full). Color the water with food coloring. Put a clear drinking straw in the bottle so that the straw goes halfway down into the bottle. Use modeling clay to seal the top of the bottle and hold the straw in place. Tape an index card to the straw. You will use the card as a scale. Make a mark on the card to show where the water level is.

Now move your thermometer to a sunny place. Does the water rise? Mark the index card to show the new water level. (You may want to mark it with an 'S' so you'll know which mark is which.) Check your thermometer at different times of the day to see how the temperature varies. You can also compare it with the weather section of your local newspaper to see if your readings match the "official" temperature.

NOW YOU SEE IT...NOW YOU DON'T

Deserts are very hot and dry places. No rain fell in the Atacama Desert in Chile from 1570 until 1971—a period of more than 400 years! If you were walking through a desert, however, you might imagine that you saw a small lake. But, when you got closer, it was gone. This is known as a mirage. The warm air near the ground in a desert causes the light from the sky to bend, creating the illusion of water.

CRICKET DEGREES

71

Did you know that crickets are nature's thermometers? Find out how to tell the temperature by cricket chirps.

Go out in the evening to a place where you know there are crickets. Single out the chirp of one cricket, and count its chirps for 14 seconds. Write down the number, and add 40 to it. The sum will tell you the temperature in degrees Fahrenheit.

STORMY WEATHER

72

You'll see nature in a whole new way when you take a walk outside in "bad" weather.

Most people make it a point to stay inside when the weather is "bad." And, most of the time, that's probably the best thing to do. But it can be interesting to go outdoors when it's rainy, snowy, foggy, or whatever. (Never go outside in a thunderstorm, snowstorm, or hailstorm. Severe weather can be dangerous.) Look for the birds and animals you usually see. How do they adapt to rain and snow? How are plants affected? Also, pay attention to what happens in nature after the rainy or snowy weather passes. What do animals do then? How do plants react? How does the sky look?

FORECAST: MORE WEATHER

73

Weather maps show more than just temperatures. Learn how to read one.

What You'll Need: A newspaper weather map

Take time to learn how to read the weather map in your local newspaper. Check the key to learn what all the different symbols and colors mean. You might see numbers that stand for high and low temperatures, lines that show warm and cold fronts, and symbols that point out where it may rain or snow. These symbols are used by meteorologists (weather experts) all over the world. Read the weather map every day for at least a week. What weather patterns do you see?

WEATHER STATION

74

Use your readings to track the weather. Then try to make predictions..

What You'll Need: Stake, small piece of peg board (about eight inches wide and one foot long), white spray paint, wire, thermometer, rain gauge (see page 42), wind sock or weather vane (see pages 39 and 40), paper to make weather chart, hygrometer (see page 45), barometer (see page 47)

In a ventilated area, paint the stake and peg board white using outdoor spray paint. Be sure to wear safety goggles and have an adult supervise. Nail the pegboard to the stake so the top of the board is one foot below the top of the stake. Use wire to fasten a thermometer and rain gauge to the pegboard. Fasten a weather vane or wind sock to the top of the stake. The north side of the wind vane's direction indicator should be on the same side as the thermometer. Find an open area with no overhanging trees or large buildings in the way. Have an adult help you dig a hole about 18 inches deep. Sink your stake into the bottom of it so that the side of the station with the thermometer is facing north. Then fill it back in and stomp the soil down firmly. Keep a weather notebook. Take readings of temperature, wind direction (and speed, if you made the wind sock), and rainfall daily. If you have a hygrometer and a barometer you can add readings of humidity and air pressure to your notebook. Compare your readings to those you see in the newspaper. See if you can predict the weather.

WEATHER FOLKTALES

75

See which old beliefs are based on fact and which are pure fancy!

What You'll Need: Notebook, pen

Our ancestors didn't have television weather forecasters, satellite weather photos, or fancy instruments to redict the weather. They had to rely on signs from nature. Some old folklore predictions are highly accurte, while others are mere superstition.

Here are some folk sayings about the weather. Which ones do you think give accurate predictions? Make ur own observations of these signs to find out, then record them in your notebook. Which do you think e more reliable: signs that rely on animals or signs that relate to the sky and clouds?

1. Red sky in the morning, sailors take warning. Red sky at night, sailor's delight.
2. Crows on the fence mean rain, while crows on the ground mean fine weather.
3. If a cow moos three times in a row, rain will come soon.
4. A ring around the sun or moon means rain is coming soon.
5. Roosters crowing at night predict rain.
6. High clouds mean fine weather, low clouds mean rain is coming.
7. Wide brown bands on a woolly bear caterpillar mean a mild winter.

ALL KINDS OF WEATHER

76

answers to all your weather questions are as close as your library.

You'll Need: One or more books on weather, paper, pen

ve you ever wondered what are the coldest, hottest, rainiest, and snowiest places on Earth? (Antarctica coldest at -128.6°F and Al Aziziyah, Libya, is the hottest at 136°F. The rainiest place in the world, i, Hawaii, gets 460 inches every year, and Washington's Mount Rainier Paradise Ranger Station, the iest place, gets 1,122 inches in the winter season.)

, have you wondered what causes tornadoes, thunder, or lightning? If so, check out some books about her and find out. Here are some good ones to look for at your library. Discover your own fun weather write them down, and share them with others.

SKYWATCHING

Since the beginning of humankind, people have gazed up at the sky and wondered: "What are the stars? What are the clouds? What is a rainbow?" Even today, with modern telescopes and satellites, there is still much we don't know about what's "up there." In this chapter you will find lots of activities to help you learn about the sky, the planets, the stars, and more. Take some time to explore, for astronomy is a field where amateurs are still making important contributions.

77

RAINBOW-MAKING

Why wait for rainbows when you can make them yourself? Here are three ways to add some color to your life.

What You'll Need: Garden hose, prism or hanging crystal ornament, a sheet of white paper, glass pan, water, metal or plastic mirror

Rainbows are caused by sunlight passing through droplets of water in the sky. Water acts just as a prism does, breaking sunlight into its many colors.

The easiest way to make rainbows is to use a garden hose with a spray attachment. On a sunny day, turn on the hose and set the sprayer to make a fine mist. Turn the hose until you can see rainbows in the mist. You might even see a double rainbow. Notice that the order of colors in the second rainbow is reversed.

If you have a prism or a crystal ornament (such as the crystals that dangle from chandeliers), you can make rainbows by holding your prism or crystal in a beam of sunlight. Turn the prism so that the rainbow falls on a white wall, or on a sheet of white paper.

The third way to make rainbows is with a metal or plastic mirror and a wide pan of water. Submerge the mirror in the water and turn it so that sunlight reflects off of it and shines on the wall. You can put up white paper to see the rainbows better. You will get wavy, ripply rainbows.

GO FLY A KITE

78

When you watch a kite sailing on the wind, you can almost imagine sailing up there yourself.

What You'll Need: Two thin, lightweight wooden sticks (36 inches and 18 inches long), string, colorful wrapping paper, tape, cloth strips

There's no better way to "see" the wind than to make and fly a kite. Here's how:

Make a cross out of two wooden sticks (one 36 inches long and the other 18 inches long), placing the shorter stick one foot from the top of the longer stick. Use string to fasten the two sticks together where they cross. Put string around the outside of the crossed sticks to make a diamond shape, and connect the string to the ends of the sticks with tape. This will make the outline of the kite. Cut wrapping paper 1½ inches larger than the outline of the kite. Put the paper over the outline. Fold the extra 1½ inch over the string and tape it down.

Tie a ball of string to the place where the sticks are joined. Tie cloth strips to another piece of string, and attach the string to the pointy end of the kite for a tail. Now you're ready to sail on the wind.

IDENTIFYING CLOUDS

79

All clouds are made of tiny droplets of water. Yet clouds come in all shapes and sizes, and bring different kinds of weather.

What You'll Need: Pen and paper

The main kinds of clouds are listed below. They're listed from the lowest to the highest in the sky. What type of clouds are in the sky right now? Keep a record of the clouds you see each day. You can draw the clouds and keep a count of how many days you see each type of cloud. Maybe you'll be able to see them all!

Low clouds (up to 6,500 feet)
Fog: Clouds in contact with the ground.
Stratus: Low sheets of clouds that form less than a mile above the earth. Like a thick blanket over the Earth, they bring dark, gray days—and, sometimes, drizzle.
Nimbostratus: A very thick, dark layer of clouds that bring rain. (*Nimbus* is Latin for rain.)
Cumulus: These are the big, white fluffy clouds that float by on sunny days. They usually mean good weather.
Stratocumulus: Cumulus clouds pressed together in layers.
Cumulonimbus: These clouds pile up into towering mountains called 'thunderheads.' They may bring thunderstorms. At their worst, they create tornadoes.

Middle clouds (6,500 to 20,000 feet)
Altocumulus: These are rows of clouds shaped like long rolls.
Altostratus: Thin, gray, layered clouds that look like a veil in front of the sun.

High clouds (20,000 to 40,000 feet)
Cirrus: These long, wispy clouds are often called 'mare's tails.' Can you guess why?
Cirrocumulus: These rows of long, thin clouds are sometimes called 'mackerel sky' because they resemble fish scales or ripples in water.
Cirrostratus: These form thin layers of high clouds that often cause a halo around the sun or moon.

CLOUDS OVERHEAD

80

A good way to remember the different clouds is to make a mobile.

What You'll Need: Poster board, scissors, plenty of cotton balls, glue, string, dowel, paint and paintbrush (optional)

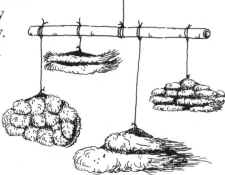

For each kind of cloud, cut its shape out of poster board. Glue cotton balls to both sides of the shape to make it look like a cloud. Make each cloud look like the real thing as much as you can. For a cumulus cloud, punch up lots of cotton balls to make it fluffy. For a cirrus cloud, stretch out the cotton balls to make them thin and wispy. You could use a little gray paint (just mix a little black into white) to make some of the clouds gray.

When all your clouds are assembled and the glue is dry, make a small hole in each one. Then tie a piece of string through each hole. Nimbostratus clouds should have the longest string, since they're closest to Earth. Cirrus clouds should have the shortest string, since they're the highest clouds.

Now tie all the clouds to a dowel. Finally, tie a piece of string around the middle of the dowel, and use it to hang your mobile.

SOLAR PRINTS

81

See what develops when you use the sun to make pictures.

What You'll Need: Some nature objects, light-sensitive paper

Gather some objects in nature that have interesting shapes, such as leaves, flowers, and twigs. Arrange some of the objects on light-sensitive paper. (You can buy this at a hobby, photography, or toy store.) Be sure to keep the paper away from the light until your objects are all arranged. Then put the paper in direct sunlight for about five minutes. Take off the objects and dip the paper in water to set the image. Lay out the paper to dry.

Solar-printed paper makes great stationery and greeting cards. Or, you can color or paint the images to make artwork.

MAKE A SUNDIAL

82

Before there were clocks, ancient people used sundials to tell time.

What You'll Need: Thin cardboard, tape, wooden board, pen or marker

Cut a piece of thin cardboard to the dimensions shown in the illustration. Tape the cardboard upright on a board. Put the sundial outdoors in a sunny place with the highest point of the triangle facing south. Starting as soon as it gets light, go to your sundial every hour on the hour, and mark where the shadow of the cardboard falls. For example, at 7 A.M., write "7 A.M." at the place where the shadow falls. Once all the hours are marked, you can use your sundial to tell time. Make sure you place your sundial in exactly the same spot each time you use it.

Can you think of ways that clocks are an improvement over sundials? The most obvious is that clocks tell time at night, too, while sundials don't. What else?

SUNRISE, SUNSET

83

You'll have to wake up early to keep track of where the sun rises and sets.

What You'll Need: Paper, pen

Get up early one morning and watch the sun rise. You'll see it best in an open area, such as a beach, lakeshore, or large, flat field. Notice where the sun rises in relation to fixed objects (such as hills or trees) near the horizon. You may want to makes notes about this. (For example, you might write: "Sun rose just to the right of the big hill.") Make a diagram showing the eastern and western horizons. Mark where you saw the sun rise. The same day (or as soon as you can), go to the same place and watch the sun set. Again, notice where the sun sets in relation to hills or trees on the horizon. Mark the spot on your diagram.

About three months later, repeat the activity. Notice where the sun rises and sets in relation to those same hills or trees. (Check your notes from last time.) Mark the spots on your diagram. Has the sun moved? The sun always rises in the east and sets in the west. It's really the Earth that has moved. As the Earth orbits the sun, it changes how much it tilts toward the sun. The result is that the sun rises and sets in different places on the horizon. Be careful not to look directly at the sun.

SUNSHINE COOKIES

84

Bring rays of sunshine to a gloomy, cloudy day with a batch of smiling sun cookies.

What You'll Need: ¾ cup butter, softened; ¾ cup sugar; 1 egg; 2¼ cups all-purpose flour; ¼ teaspoon salt; grated peel of ½ lemon; 1 teaspoon frozen lemonade concentrate, thawed; Lemonade Royal Icing 6 tablespoons frozen lemonade concentrate, thawed; 3¼ cups sifted powdered sugar; 3 tablespoons meringue powder); cookie sheets; 3-inch round cookie cutter; 1 egg, beaten; thin pretzel sticks; yellow paste food color; water; gummy fruit candy; black licorice strings

Beat butter and sugar in large bowl at high speed of electric mixer until fluffy. Add egg; beat well. Combine flour, salt, and lemon peel in medium bowl. Add to butter mixture. Stir in 1 teaspoon lemonade concentrate. Refrigerate for 2 hours.

Prepare the icing: Combine 6 tablespoons of frozen lemonade concentrate with sifted powdered sugar and meringue powder in large bowl. Beat at high speed of electric mixer until smooth. Cover; let stand at room temperature.

Preheat oven to 350°F. Grease cookie sheets.

Roll dough on floured surface to ⅛-inch thickness. Using cookie cutter, cut out cookies and place on cookie sheets. Brush cookies with beaten egg. Arrange pretzel sticks around the edge of the cookies to represent sunshine rays; press gently into cookies. Bake 10 minutes or until lightly browned. Remove to wire racks; cool completely.

Add food color to icing. Add water, 1 tablespoon at a time, to icing, until thick but pourable consistency. Turn cookies over; spoon icing in centers and spread it out over cookies.

Decorate cookies with gummy fruit candy and licorice to make a face like the one in the illustration. Let stand one hour or until dry. Makes about 3 dozen cookies.

OUR SUN

There are millions of stars in our galaxy, and the sun is just one of them. The sun, however, is the center of our solar system, and all of the planets in our solar system revolve around the sun. The diameter of the sun is about 865,000 miles, which is more than 100 times that of the earth. More than one million planets the size of the Earth would fit into the sun.

SEE IT SAFELY

85

A solar eclipse is a rare event that everyone wants to see, but looking at the sun is dangerous. Use this eclipse viewer instead.

What You'll Need: Two pieces of cardboard, pin or nail to poke hole

A solar eclipse happens when the moon comes between the Earth and the sun. The moon blocks out the sun, and the Earth gets dark in the daytime. But actually looking at an eclipse—or looking at the sun on any day—can cause blindness, because the sun's light is so strong. Here is how to make a viewer that will allow you to see an eclipse safely.

Get two pieces of cardboard, each about the size of a piece of notebook paper or a little smaller. Poke a small hole in the middle of one piece of cardboard. At the time of an eclipse, hold the piece with the hole up to the sun, with the other piece of cardboard beneath it, as shown. Look at the second piece of cardboard. An image of the eclipse will be projected onto it. You should see a circle with a 'bite' taken out of it; the bite is the shadow of the moon in front of the sun.

HOT DOG!

86

You know the sun is hot, but you didn't know it was this hot! Make a solar oven.

What You'll Need: A cylindrical oatmeal box, sharp knife, aluminum foil, hot dog

Have a grownup cut an oatmeal box in half lengthwise. Line half of the box with aluminum foil. (Put the shiny side up.) Take your solar oven outside and put it in the bright, hot sun. The aluminum foil will cause the sunlight to reflect from one side of the 'oven' to the other, making it really hot. Put a hot dog in your solar oven, and watch it sizzle!

WHEEL OF TIME

87

What time is it in Sydney, Australia, right now? With this activity, you'll be able to tell the time all over the world.

What You'll Need: Large piece of poster board, large piece of cardboard, yardstick, markers, thumbtack

The world is divided into 24 time zones. When it's midnight in one time zone, on the side of the Earth opposite from that spot, it's noon.

Cut a piece of poster board into a large circle. Draw lines that divide the circle into 24 equal-size wedge-shaped pieces.

Write one hour of the day in each time zone. Start with 2 A.M. and go from there. Write the hours near the center of the circle. Write them in order, of course, and be sure to write whether each time is A.M. or P.M.

Put a thumbtack in the center of the circle, and attach the circle to a big piece of cardboard.

Now, use the table to write the name of each place next to its correct time zone outside the circle's edge on the cardboard.

Check your watch. What time is it where you are? Turn the circle until that time lines up with the name of a city in your time zone.

Now you can read your time-zone chart to tell what time it is right now in other cities all over the world.

1 A.M.	central Pacific Ocean
2 A.M.	Honolulu, Hawaii
3 A.M.	Anchorage, Alaska
4 A.M.	Los Angeles, California
5 A.M.	Denver, Colorado
6 A.M.	Chicago, Illinois
7 A.M.	New York, New York
8 A.M.	Caracas, Venezuela
9 A.M.	Rio de Janeiro, Brazil
10 A.M.	mid-Atlantic Ocean
11 A.M.	Atlantic Ocean
12 P.M.	London, England
1 P.M.	Paris, France
2 P.M.	Cairo, Egypt
3 P.M.	Moscow, Russia
4 P.M.	Dubai, United Arab Emirates
5 P.M.	Karachi, Pakistan
6 P.M.	Indian Ocean
7 P.M.	Bangkok, Thailand
8 P.M.	Beijing, China
9 P.M.	Tokyo, Japan
10 P.M.	Sydney, Australia
11 P.M.	western Pacific Ocean
12 A.M	Auckland, New Zealand

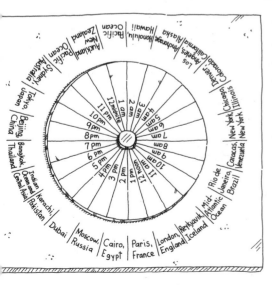

PUT THE SUN TO WORK

88

Are you thirsty? Take advantage of solar energy and learn how to brew refreshing sun tea.

What You'll Need: Half-gallon glass jar with lid, water, herbal tea bags, ice cubes

Fill a half-gallon glass jar with cold water. Remember to be careful when handling glass. Put in four or fiv teabags and put the lid on the jar. (You can use more or fewer teabags, depending on how strong you like your tea.) Let the jar sit outdoors in direct sunlight for several hours to brew the tea. When it's ready, remov the tea bags. Pour your sun tea into a glass and add ice. Put the jar in the refrigerator to keep the rest of the tea fresh.

THE TOAD IN THE MOON?

89

There are lots of stories that try to explain the shadows on the moon. Now it's your turn to make up a legend.

People in different parts of the world have had different ideas about just who, or what, is "in the moon." In the United States, we look at the shadows on the full moon and say it is "the man in the moon"' In Germany, people say that man was sent there for something he did wrong. In Africa, the Masai people say it's "the *woman* in the moon." And in China, they say it's a rabbit or a toad.

Take a good look at the full moon. What do *you* see there? Write a story telling who, or what, is in the moon, and how it got there. Then see what stories your friends can tell.

TIME FLIES

90

Learn about the parts of the moon's cycle with a lunar phases flipbook.

What You'll Need: 16 plain white index cards, black marker, heavy-duty stapler

The moon is another great example of nature's cycles. Every 29½ days, the moon goes through a complete cycle. The moon begins the cycle being invisible. This happens when the moon comes between the sun and the Earth, so that sunlight only shines on the backside of the moon where we can't see it. As the moon moves around the Earth, we see more of the sunlit part of the moon. Halfway through the cycle we see a full moon. At that time, the whole face of the moon is lighted up by the sun. Then we see less and less of the moon until finally it is invisible again.

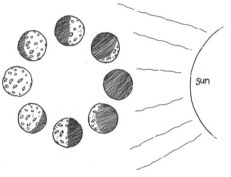

On 16 index cards, draw the phases as shown on this page. Draw each "moon" on the right half of the card. Stack the cards in order, with the first one on top of the stack. Staple all the cards together on the left side, or just hold the cards together firmly. With your other hand, flip through the stack to see the moon's phases.

GOING THROUGH A PHASE

91

Make a model of the sun, Earth, and moon to show the phases of the moon.

What You'll Need: Pencil, plastic foam ball, lamp without a shade, dark room

Stick a pencil into a plastic foam ball. The ball stands for the moon. Use the pencil as a handle.

Darken the room, and turn on a lamp that doesn't have a shade. Put the lamp at eye level in the middle of the room. Now face the lamp. The lamp is the sun and you are the Earth! Hold the plastic foam ball directly between you and the light. The side of the ball that is facing you will be dark. This is called the new moon.

Now, hold the ball at arm's length while you turn in place. You might want to hold the ball above your head so the light can always reach it as you turn. Watch the ball. It will go through the phases of the moon as different sides of the ball are hit. When you are between the lamp and the ball, with the light shining completely on the ball, the ball will look like a full moon.

STAR GAZING

92

Its easy to teach yourself how to recognize the stars and constellations.

What You'll Need: Star chart, flashlight, piece of red cellophane

First get a star chart and learn about the night sky. You can find one in many books at the library. Then, on a clear night, go outdoors and see if you can find the constellations in the sky. The stars move throughout the year, so you'll see different constellations at different times of year.

The starting point for star-gazing is usually the North Star, also called Polaris. It's the only one that does not move. To find the North Star, find the Little Dipper. The last star on its handle is the North Star. Another way to find the North Star is to locate the Big Dipper and trace an imaginary line from the two stars in the dipper's front edge, leading up from the dipper. The North Star is along this line. Once you've found the North Star, try to locate the other constellations. Use a flashlight to refer to your star chart. (Cover the flashlight with red cellophane so you can still see the stars when you look back up at the sky.)

IT'S RAINING STARS

93

Turn your umbrella into your own private planetarium.

What You'll Need: Black umbrella, white chalk, star chart

Do this activity on a crystal clear night when the moon is either invisible or very small. If you can, go to a place where there are few or no human-made lights.

Ask an adult if you can mark up an old, black umbrella with chalk. Open the umbrella and hold it over your head. Point the tip of the umbrella at the North Star. (Use a star chart to find the North Star, or ask an adult to help you.) Look up at the underside of the umbrella. You may see the stars shining through. Use white chalk to mark on the umbrella each place where you see a star. (This will be easier if someone else holds the umbrella for you.) If you can't see the stars through the umbrella, just look in the sky and mark the stars in the same positions as you see them in the sky. When you've marked all the stars you can see, take the umbrella inside. Compare your marks to a star chart. What stars and constellations did you mark? Draw lines connecting the constellations, and label them with their names.

STAR THEATER

94

You'll be the star when you learn the shapes of some constellations and put on a show for your family!

What You'll Need: Empty steel cans (such as soup or coffee cans), pliers, tracing paper, book of constellations, pen, scissors, pin, masking tape, hammer, thin finishing nail, flashlight, black cloth (optional)

You may need an adult's help with this project. Clean the cans and use pliers to flatten any sharp points. Lay the end of the can on the tracing paper and draw circles with a pencil. Lay the marked tracing paper on a picture of a constellation in a book and trace a constellation inside of each circle, using dots to represent stars. If a constellation won't fit in the circle, you can try drawing it free hand. Cut out the circles, and use a pin to poke a hole where each star is marked. Then turn each circle over so the constellation is backward, and tape one to the closed end of the steel can. Use a hammer and a thin finishing nail to punch a hole through each pin hole. (Always be careful when using a hammer!) Remove the paper.

Write the name of each constellation on a piece of masking tape and attach each piece of masking tape to the can it represents. This is so you can remember which constellation is which. Shine a flashlight into the open end of the can to shine the constellation on the ceiling. You can shroud the open end of the can in black cloth to shut out excess light when you put on a star show for your family.

STAR LIGHT, STAR BRIGHT

On a clear night, you can probably see only 3,000 stars out of the millions of stars in the sky. Some stars appear much brighter than others. This is because they are either larger, have a stronger light, or are closer to the Earth than other stars. The star nearest to the Earth, other than our sun, is Proxima Centauri, which is about 25 trillion miles away!

PEAS IN SPACE!

95

Or would you rather have the walnuts? Make a true scale model of the solar system.

What You'll Need: A ball that is about 27 inches in diameter (such as a beach ball), five peas, one orange, one tangerine, two walnuts, tape measure, a large open space

You've probably seen lots of drawings and diagrams of the solar system. But, to make the drawings fit on a piece of paper, the artists have to draw the planets closer together than they really are. In this activity, you'll make a scale model of the solar system. You'll be surprised to see how much bigger some planets are than others, and how far apart some of them are.

Make your model in a large open space that will represent, uh, space! Put a beach ball or other large ball at one end of the space. The ball is the sun. Place the other objects as follows. (Remember to measure each planet from the sun.)

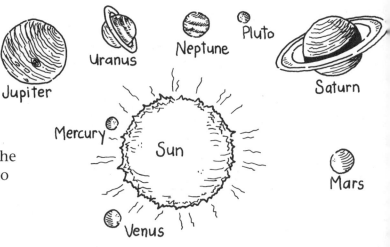

Planet	Object	Distance from the Sun
Mercury	Pea	1¾ inches
Venus	Pea	3¼ inches
Earth	Pea	4½ inches
Mars	Pea	7 inches
Jupiter	Orange	2 feet
Saturn	Tangerine	3 feet, 7 inches
Uranus	Walnut	7 feet, 3 inches
Neptune	Walnut	11 feet, 4 inches
Pluto	Pea	14 feet, 10 inches

ASTROLABE

96

Learn how to measure the position of stars with this simple instrument.

What You'll Need: String, plastic protractor, weight (washer, rock, or fishing weight), pen and paper

When scientists describe the position of a star in the sky, they measure its position relative to the horizon. An instrument called an astrolabe measures how high above the horizon the star is in degrees.

Tie a 12-inch piece of string to the hole in the middle of the crossbar on the protractor. Tie a weight to the other end. Hold the protractor so that the curved part is down and the zero degree mark is closest to you. Sit on the ground and look along the flat edge of the protractor with your eye at the zero mark. Point the flat edge at the star whose position you want to measure. Once you have the star at the end of your sight, hold the string against the side of the protractor. Note which degree mark the string crosses. Write this down in your notebook. This number tells you how many degrees above the horizon your star is.

Take readings for several stars. Return every 30 minutes and take new readings. Notice the pattern in which the stars seem to move across the sky as the earth turns.

STELLAR STORIES

97

This is your chance to wish upon a star.

What You'll Need: Paper, pen, markers

In ancient times, people all over the world made up stories to explain what the stars are or where they came from. Some people believed that when people died, they became stars. If you didn't know that stars were giant, balls of flaming gas millions of miles away, what would *you* think? Be creative, and make up a story to explain the stars. What are they? Why are there so many of them? Why do they twinkle? Make an illustrated story book that tells your "star story." And don't forget to give your story a title!

THE SKY IS FALLING!

98

There is nothing as breathtaking as a shooting star. Find out when and where you can scan the skies for meteor showers.

What You'll Need: A clear night sky—and maybe an afternoon nap

Space is chock-full of tiny planetlike spheres known as asteroids. That is, they're tiny by space standards; a very small asteroid *might* fit inside your house. Millions of fragments from asteroids can fall into the Earth's atmosphere. When one of these fragments comes close to Earth and burns up, it makes a streak of light that can be seen in the night sky. This streak is called a meteor or a shooting star.

By the way, most of these fragments burn up completely in the atmosphere. But once in a while one lands on Earth. When that happens, it's called a meteorite.

Skywatchers have learned that there are certain times and places when lots of meteors can be seen. These events are called meteor showers, and they're worth staying up late for. (The best time to see meteors is after midnight, and the best place is away from city lights.) Here are the times and places of some of the biggest meteor showers. Use a star map to find the places listed.

When	Where
January 1-3	Eastern sky, between Boötes and Draco. This is called the Quadrantid meteor shower, and it's the flashiest one of the year!
April 20-22	Northeastern sky, between Vega and Hercules.
May 4-6	Eastern sky, to the southwest of the Square of Pegasus.
August 10-13	Northeastern sky, around Perseus. Called the Perseids, this is the most famous meteor shower and is second only to the Quadrantids in the number of meteors.
October 20-23	Eastern sky, between Orion and Gemini.
November 3-10	Northeastern sky, between Taurus, Auriga, and Perseus.
December 10-12	Eastern sky, in Gemini.

TRAVEL TO OUTER SPACE

99

Imagine what it would be like to float among the planets, stars, and comets!

What You'll Need: Scissors, cardboard or heavy paper, decorations (paint, aluminum foil, or glitter), pin, thread or nylon line, two dowel rods or sticks

If you hang a space mobile in your room, you can look up and imagine you're up there.

Cut out and color shapes to make planets, stars, spaceships, and other objects found in outer space. Use interesting materials such as glow-in-the-dark paint, aluminum foil, and glitter. Also use your imagination, and include anything you think might be found in space: alien monsters? giant doughnuts? It's *your* universe!

Next use a pin to make a small hole in each shape you made. Tie a piece of thread or nylon line through each hole. Next, cross one dowel rod over the other at a right angle. Tie the dowels together, then tie your shapes to the dowels. Tie different shapes at different heights. Finally, tie a strong thread or piece of nylon line around the dowels to hang your mobile. You've got your head in the stars!

LOST IN SPACE?

100

There is so much to learn about space and the solar system! Explore the galaxy without even leaving your home.

What You'll Need: One or more books about space, paper, pen

What are comets made of? Why do the planets in our solar system orbit around the sun? What is a galaxy? How long would it take to travel to Pluto? You can learn the answers to these questions and a lot more about space by reading about it. Find some books at your library. After you've learned all about space, write a story in which you pretend you are a space traveler. Put some of the things you learned in your story, to make it seem more real.

PLANTS ALL AROUND US

If you've ever walked through a garden, some woods, or a park, you're probably familiar with a wide variety of plants. The activities in this chapter will help you learn more about the plants you see without causing damage to their habitat. You'll also find out about seeds, fruits, herbs, and how to grow plants of all kinds—including the carnivorous Venus Flytrap!

NATURAL BOOKMARKS

101

Create truly individual bookmarks using the beauty of plants. These make great gifts for your favorite bookworms.

What You'll Need: Pressed plants (see page 75), 2×6½-inch strip of colored paper or tagboard, craft glue, glitter (optional), clear Contact® paper, scissors

Lay your pressed plants out on a strip of tagboard or colored paper and arrange them until you have a design you like. Remove the plants and dot glue wherever you want to stick the plants. Lay the plants on the glue and allow to dry. If you like, spread some more glue on and sprinkle on glitter. Shake the excess glitter off onto a paper. Allow the glue to dry.

Cut a piece of clear Contact® paper about 4×6½ inches. Carefully peel off the backing and lay it flat, sticky-side up, on a table. (You may need someone to help you with this.) Turn the tagboard over so the decorated side is down and lay it in the middle of the Contact® paper Fold the rest of the Contact® paper over to cover the back. Trim the ends, leaving a small margin of Contact® paper. If you have access to a laminating machine you can laminate your bookmarks instead of using Contact® paper.

MAKE A PLANT PRESS

102

A plant press is easy to make and even easier to use.

What You'll Need: Two thin boards (about 8"×10"), saw, corrugated cardboard, utility knife, newspaper, scissors, paper towels, nylon webbing straps (one-inch wide), four D-rings, plants

Have an adult help you cut two thin boards to the size you want the press to be, about the size of a paper towel. Then, using the utility knife, cut sheets of sturdy corrugated cardboard the same size as your boards. Cut newspaper sheets twice the size of your paper towels and fold them in half.

To build the press: Lay down one board first, then a cardboard sheet, then two paper towels to act as a blotter, next a folded sheet of newspaper. Then add another sheet of cardboard and keep going in the same order. The last things to go on should be one last piece of cardboard, then the other board. Cut two straps of nylon long enough to go around the press twice. Slip the end of each strap through two D-rings, fold the end over, and sew in place. Ask an adult to melt the other end in a flame to prevent fraying. Wrap a strap once around the press and slip the free end through both D-rings. Turn the strap back, slip it through the bottom D-ring, and pull the strap to tighten.

To press plants: Lay them inside the folded newspapers and spread them out so they don't overlap. Arrange leaves and petals so that they lay flat. Build up your press as described above, using as many cardboard sheets and paper towel blotters as you need. Squeeze the layers together, strap the press tightly, and put it in a warm place for a week or more to dry. Then you can use your pressed plants to make things like bookmarks (see page 74) or stationery (see page 76).

WHAT IS A SEED?

All flowering plants reproduce by the use of seeds. Inside flowers, there are male parts called stamens, which produce pollen, and female parts called carpels, which form eggs. Once an egg is fertilized by the pollen, a seed is formed. Some plants don't produce flowers, but do make seeds (like pine trees). Other plants (like ferns) don't make seeds at all. They create new plants by making spores. You can see clusters of spores (which look like dots) on the underside of fern leaves.

103

CATCH THE SUN

Create shimmery stationery or hang your creations as sun-catchers.

What You'll Need: Colored writing paper, scissors, newspaper, waxed paper, pressed plants (see page 75), ironing board and iron, pinking shears (optional)

Fold a piece of colored writing paper in half and cut it to the size you want. Unfold it and lay it out on a sheet of newspaper. Tear off a piece of waxed paper and lay it over your cut paper. Arrange the pressed plants on the half of the paper that will be the front of your card until you have a design you like. Tear off another sheet of waxed paper and lay it on the first. Now *carefully* slide the waxed paper stack off of the paper and onto the newspaper. Cover with another sheet of newspaper and carry the whole thing to an ironing board. Have an adult help you use a warm iron to fuse the waxed paper together. When it is fused, trim the waxed paper to fit the colored paper and fold in half with the colored paper inside. The arrangement of plants will form the front of the card. If you like, trim the edges with pinking shears.

For a sun-catcher: Take the fused waxed paper and cut around the flowers. Punch a hole in the top and hang your creation up in a window.

CYCLE OF LIFE

104

A small plant can demonstrate nature's ability to recycle.

What You'll Need: Plant, large jar with lid

Water a small potted plant well. Then put the plant—pot and all—in a big, wide-mouthed jar and put the lid on tightly. Put the jar where it will get sunlight, and leave it there for 30 days. (Be careful that it doesn't get too hot or you could hurt the plant.) Observe what happens in the jar. Droplets of water will collect on the jar and drip down into the soil so the plant can use the water again. Because this is a self-contained system, the plant can live "on its own" inside the sealed jar.

THAT'S A LOT OF PLANTS!

There are close to 300,000 species of plants that scientists have already named. These plants include mosses that grow close to the ground and huge trees that tower hundreds of feet high. There are plants growing in almost part of the world today—even in the most difficult climates.

ROOT VIEW BOX

105

Plants grow two ways—up out of the soil and down into the ground. Use this special box to watch how roots grow.

What You'll Need: Half-gallon milk carton; scissors; sheet of glass, clear acrylic, or stiff clear plastic packaging; craft glue or tape; potting soil; seeds of vegetables with large roots; pan or tray; cardboard

Cut off the top of the milk carton and punch a few holes in the bottom for drainage. Cut a window in the side, leaving a ½ inch margin all the way around the window. Have an adult cut a sheet of glass or clear acrylic to fit the window inside the box. Another option is to check all the plastic packaging that is thrown away in your house for a piece of stiff, clear plastic that will fit the window. Glue or tape the plastic to the inside of box. Let it dry completely.

Now fill the box with potting soil. Plant seeds of carrots, radishes, or other root vegetables right up against the side of the box where the window is. Set the carton on a pan or tray to catch extra water, then water the seeds well. Put a bit of cardboard under the bottom of the box on the side opposite the window. This will tilt the box slightly, so the roots will grow right up against the window. Check the plant's growth to see how the roots are developing. Be sure to give your plants enough water and light. If you want to do this as a science-fair project, be sure to plant the seeds at least eight weeks ahead of time.

I SEE THE LIGHT

106

No matter what, plants always grow toward light!

What You'll Need: Plastic cup, potting soil, pinto beans, scissors, cardboard, shoe box

First, punch a few drainage holes in the bottom of a cup, add some potting soil, and plant a few pinto beans. Water the beans and put them in a warm place. Next tape two pieces of cardboard into a shoe box to make a maze, as shown. Cut a hole in one end of the shoe box. Keep the soil moist until the beans sprout, then put the cup in the shoe box. Put the lid on the shoe box.

Take the lid off the box every day to look at the bean plants and to water them as needed. Always make sure to put the lid back. Which way are the plants growing? See how long it takes them to grow out of the hole, into the light.

FREE PLANTS!

107

Get new plants for free by taking cuttings of old ones.

What You'll Need: Houseplants (such as African violet, begonia, or geranium), knife, small bottle, flower pots, potting soil, perlite or vermiculite (optional)

With the help of an adult, take a knife and cut a section of a houseplant stem with five or six leaves on it. Trim away any flowers and cut off the bottom three leaves. Then fill a small bottle with water and place the stem of the cutting into the water. The remaining leaves will hold the cutting in place. Put the bottle near a sunny window but not in direct sunlight. Add water to the bottle as needed to keep the stem in water.

After a few weeks the cutting should have long roots and be ready for planting. Fill a small flower pot with potting soil up to about ½ inch from the top. Dig a hole large enough for the roots. Lower the cutting in and carefully cover the roots.

You can also start cuttings in vermiculite or perlite, which are heat-expanded rocks. You can buy them at a garden store. Fill a small jar with vermiculite or perlite and add water. Take a cutting as described above. Poke a hole in the vermiculite or perlite and lower the cutting into it. Allow roots to grow for three weeks, adding water as needed. After the roots have grown, pot up in potting soil.

VEGETABLE IN A BOTTLE

108

This trick will mystify everyone—but it takes a lot of patience!

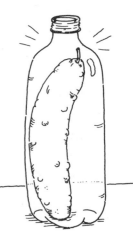

What You'll Need: Clear plastic bottle with a narrow mouth (such as a soft drink bottle), garden vegetable plant (such as cucumber or zucchini), wooden box (optional)

Find someone friendly who has a vegetable garden and who is willing to help you. Watch for a garden plant to blossom and set fruit. Cucumbers, zucchini, or gourds work well for this. Slip the tiny vegetable—still attached to the stem—into the neck of a plastic bottle. Be careful not to break the stem. Make sure the bottle is shaded under the leaves of the plant, or cover the bottle with a wooden box to keep the sun from heating the bottle too much. Now wait for the vegetable to grow. Once it's big enough to nearly fill the bottle, cut the stem and go show your friends. See if they can figure out how the vegetable got in the bottle. Then you can cut away the bottle to get the vegetable out.

UNFRIENDLY FOLIAGE

109

Not all plants are safe to touch or taste. Make a poster showing which plants to stay away from.

What You'll Need: Plant reference books, poster board, markers or paint

People have found ways to use many kinds of plants. Many plants are used for food. Others—like rubber trees and aloe—are used to make products. Some have beautiful flowers, and some smell good. But there are a few plants that are nothing but trouble to humans. If you've ever had poison ivy, you know just what we're talking about!

At the library, find a book that tells about poisonous plants. (Poisonous plants include Holly Berries, Locoweed, Poison Ivy, Poison Oak, Poison Sumac, Potato leaves and stem, Rhubarb leaves.) Make a poster that tells which plants are poisonous and shows what they look like. See if your school or public library would like to display the poster.

SEED JEWELRY

110

Create a fashion statement by making jewelry from nature's treasures.

What You'll Need: Large seeds from the wild or from the grocery store (such as sunflower seeds, watermelon seeds, etc.), sieve, paper, needle, strong thread or dental floss, barrel-type jewelry fasteners (from a crafts store), earring backs, strong craft glue, spray acrylic (optional)

First you will need to collect your seeds. Save seeds from watermelons, cantaloupes, apples, pumpkins, squash, and anything else you can find that has large seeds. Wash them in a sieve and let them dry thoroughly. If they're in season, you can also find some ears of "Indian" corn and remove the colorful corn seeds.

When you have enough seeds, lay them out on white paper and think about how you'd like to arrange them. Soak the seeds you plan to use for a few hours until soft. Use a plain sewing needle and strong thread or unwaxed dental floss to string your seeds. (Always be careful when handling a needle!) You can make necklaces from single, double, or even triple strands of seeds. Tie barrel-type jewelry fasteners to the ends of your string for shorter necklaces, chokers, or bracelets. For earrings, glue seeds into flower shapes on earring backs. If you like, you can add shine to your finished jewelry with clear acrylic spray. Ask an adult to help you use the spray, and be sure to work in a well-ventilated area.

DIRT CUPS

111

If worms live in dirt, where do gummy worms live? Make a model of a worm's home in the soil—a model that's good enough to eat!

What You'll Need: Plastic cup; gummy worms; ice cream; 4 chocolate sandwich cookies, crushed; 1 tablespoon chocolate syrup; plastic flowers (optional)

Put two or three gummy worms on the bottom of a plastic cup. Cover "worms" with a scoop of your favorite flavor of ice cream. Top with crushed cookies and chocolate syrup to make the cup look like a pot of soil. Then feel free to decorate with additional gummy worms or plastic flowers.

SPECKLED PLANTS

112

Make a mosaic to show the many colors of plants.

What You'll Need: A variety of dried beans, seeds, and peas; cardboard, poster board, or plywood; marker or crayon; craft glue

Start with a trip to a grocery store. (If possible, go to one that sells a wide variety of beans and peas in bulk, so you can buy just a handful of each.) Check out all the different kinds of dried (not canned) beans and peas. You should find beans in black, red, brown, white, and speckles. You'll find bright green peas and light green lima beans. Lentils come in many colors, including pink! Don't forget to check out seeds, too: tiny black poppy seeds, stripy sunflower seeds, green pumpkin seeds, and whatever else strikes your fancy.

Collect as many different shapes, sizes, and colors of beans and seeds as you can. Then use them to make a mosaic. Make a drawing on a piece of cardboard, poster board, or plywood. Then glue on beans and seeds to fill in your drawing.

SEED COLLECTIONS

113

You'll be surprised by how interesting and attractive seeds can be!

What You'll Need: Seeds, small bottles or clear film canisters, masking tape, flower guide, pen, small glass bottles, strip of thin wood, sandpaper, varnish, craft glue

Begin collecting seeds around your house. Look for garden flowers, grasses, and weeds that have gone to seed. Gather seeds from fruits and vegetables in the kitchen. Use small bottles or clear film canisters to put seeds in. (You can get film canisters from a photo developer.) Use masking tape to label the bottles. A flower guide can help you identify the plants. When collecting seeds from wild plants, be sure to get permission from the property owner. Never collect plants or plant parts from state and national forests.

When you have 10 or 20 different kinds of seeds collected, you can use tiny glass bottles to display them. (Always be careful when handling glass.) Ask an adult to help you sand and varnish a 1-inch-wide strip of wood. Glue the bottles in a row on the wood strip. Put a different kind of seed in each bottle and screw the caps on tightly. Glue a label under each sample to identify it.

114 MINI-GREENHOUSES

Winter is the perfect time to start seeds indoors for a spring garden.

What You'll Need: Small pots or containers (such as yogurt containers or soup cans), potting soil, water, flower or vegetable seeds, plastic bags

Punch some holes in the bottom of your containers for drainage. Fill them with potting soil. Use sterile soil so the seedlings won't catch a fungal disease called "damping off." Wet the soil and set the containers aside to drain.

Plant only two or three seeds in each container. As a rule, plant the seed no deeper than four times its diameter. (Plant lettuce seeds on top of the soil because they need light to sprout.) Put each container in a plastic bag, such as the kind that groceries use for fruits and vegetables. Gather up the mouth of the bag and blow into it, then tie off the top with a twist-tie to make a miniature greenhouse. Set the greenhouse in a warm room. Once you see sprouts, put your greenhouses in a sunny window. It's also a good idea to take the greenhouses outdoors on warm days where they can get more sun for a few hours each day.

The first green "leaves" on your seedlings are called "seed leaves." They are not true leaves, but parts of the seed. Wait until the seedlings have at least four true leaves and are tall and strong before transplanting them outdoors.

DO PLANTS BREATHE? 115

Even though plants don't breathe like you do, they still need air.

What You'll Need: Plant, petroleum jelly

Too see how plants take air in and out, get a small plant with lots of leaves. Cover the *tops* of five leaves with a heavy coat of petroleum jelly. Then cover the *undersides* of five other leaves with a heavy coat of petroleum jelly.

Look at the plants each day for a week. What happens? What does this tell you about how plants take air in and out? There are openings on the undersides of leaves. Air moves in and out of those openings, allowing a plant to exchange gases.

GOURD PUPPET

116

Pick out some funny-shaped gourds, make puppets, and put on a show!

What You'll Need: Small gourd, knife, spoon, paint, fabric, needle, thread

You can pick gourds fresh from a garden or find them in markets during the fall or winter.

To Make a Gourd Finger Puppet: Using the long, curved top of the gourd as the nose, paint features for the face. Have an adult help you cut a hole in the bottom of the puppet's "head" and scoop out the contents with a spoon. Allow the gourd to dry, then use your finger as the puppet's neck.

To Make a Gourd Hand Puppet: Turn the gourd upside-down and use the long, curved part as the neck. Draw a funny face on the "head." You can dress your puppet with clothes sewn together from fabric scraps.

PLANT YOUR SOCKS?

117

Imagine what would happen if your socks started to sprout.

What You'll Need: Pair of old, worn-out tube socks, shallow aluminum foil pan, water

Get a pair of old tube socks, and put them on over your shoes. Go for a walk through a field of tall grass and weeds. (The best time to do this is in the early fall, but you can try it in spring and summer, too.) Carefully take off the socks once they are covered with seeds. When you get home, put the socks in a shallow aluminum foil pan with a little water in the bottom. There should be just enough water to make the socks wet—no more. Put the pan in a place indoors where it will get plenty of light, and keep those socks moist. In a few days, the seeds that stuck to your socks will begin to sprout. Let your sock garden grow for awhile to see what kinds of plants you have.

118 GROWING HERBS

Food tastes extra-special when prepared with fresh herbs!

What You'll Need: Flower pots, potting soil, water, herb seeds (basil, sage, mint, parsley, thyme, and marjoram), plastic wrap

Fill some medium-sized flower pots (about four to six inches) with potting soil. Water the soil completely and let the pots drain. Sprinkle a few herb seeds on top and press them into the soil. Large seeds, such as parsley, may have to be soaked for a few hours before planting to help them sprout. Cover the pots with plastic wrap and set them in a warm place to sprout. Herb seeds may take two weeks to sprout.

Once the seedlings are up, set the pots in a sunny window. Remove the plastic wrap and lay it loosely on top of the pots to help keep moisture in but allow air to circulate. Remove it completely when the plants have several true leaves. Water the plants when the soil feels a little dry. Let it dry out completely once or twice in the fall. Use a plant mister or spray bottle to mist the plants weekly.

HERB PILLOW 119

See what "sweet" dreams this pillow of herbs will bring you.

What You'll Need: Fabric scraps, scissors, fabric paints, paintbrush, needle and thread, herbs, cookie sheet, ribbon (optional)

Cut two squares of fabric to the size you want. Paint a flowery design on one of the squares with fabric paint and let it dry. Put the two squares together with the painted side in. With help from an adult, sew the edges of the square with a ¼-inch seam, leaving a 2-inch opening. Turn the pillow right-side out. Now, choose some herbs for your pillow. Tradition holds that chamomile, catnip, and hops bring about peaceful sleep. Have an adult help you dry the herbs so you can fill the pillow. To dry herbs, place them on a cookie sheet. Bake in a 350°F oven for 15 minutes or until herbs are dry enough to crumble. When you fill the pillow, don't stuff it full; it should be somewhat flat. Sew the opening shut. Tie a ribbon in a bow and sew it to the pillow, or decorate any other way you like with ribbons.

A SPOT OF TEA

120

Many herbs and flowers can be used to make delicious tea.

What You'll Need: Herbs or flowers that make good tea (chamomile, red clover, or mint), hot water, strainer, sugar or honey (optional)

Try growing your own herbs for tea. Mint grows fast and can be grown indoors under a full-spectrum "grow light." Or you can harvest wild herbs and flowers for tea. Just be sure an adult goes with you to help you make sure that the herbs you're harvesting are okay to eat. Red clover is often found growing wild, and it makes a good tea.

Make tea from fresh herbs and flowers right after you gather them. Ask an adult to pour boiling water over them and let them steep for about five minutes. Then pour the tea through a strainer to remove the herbs. Add a little sugar or honey, if you like.

ONION/GARLIC BRAIDS

121

After harvesting onions or garlic, make them into braids.

What You'll Need: Onions or garlic with tops intact, newspaper, string

Begin with whole, undamaged onions or garlic. If you dig them from your garden be sure to clean off as much dirt as you can. Do not cut off the tops because you will need these to braid. Lay the onions or garlic out on newspapers in a cool, dry, sheltered place until the tops are dry.

When they are ready, take three of your onions and braid the tops together for a few inches. Lay two more onions alongside right where the braid stops, separate their tops into the three strands you are braiding, and braid for another few inches. Add two more onions, and keep going. When you have about two feet of onions in your braid, stop adding onions. Braid the remainder of the tops together and tie the braid off with string. Loop the braid over onto itself and tie the loop with more string. Hang the braid in the kitchen, preferably from a hook on the ceiling, where air will circulate around the onions.

Make a garlic braid the same way, but leave only an inch or two between the bulbs. Garlic bulbs are much smaller than onions so they can be laid closer together.

NATURAL DYES

122

Before there were chemical dyes, people had to make their own dyes from plant materials. Try your hand at dyeing a shirt or bandanna.

What You'll Need: Wool or cotton material to dye, laundry detergent, a variety of colorful plant material (see suggestions below), knife, glass bowl, water, old saucepans, sieve, alum (available in the spice rack at grocery stores), dye

You'll need an adult to help you with the cutting and boiling in this project.

1. Wash cotton or wool material in plain detergent with no fabric softener.

2. Cut up your plant materials. Chop up or crush hard materials such as roots. Soak them overnight in a glass or enamel bowl with just enough water to cover them.

3. Pour the contents of the bowl into a stainless steel pan. Bring to a boil on the stove and simmer gently for about one hour. Check it frequently and add water when needed.

4. Strain the dye through a sieve to remove plant material. Allow the liquid to cool.

5. Measure the liquid. For every quart of dye, add one half ounce of alum (about one tablespoon). Alum is a *mordant*. That means it helps set the dye.

6. Wet your fabric and wring it out, then put it in the steel pan with your dye. Put the pan on the stove and simmer slowly until the fabric is just a little darker than you want it. (The fabric will look lighter when it dries.) Remember that natural colors will be soft, not bright.

7. Move the pan to the sink and pour everything through a strainer. Run a little cold water over your fabric to cool and rinse it, wring it out, and hang it up to dry outdoors where the drips won't hurt anything. Here are some of the colors you can make from common plants.

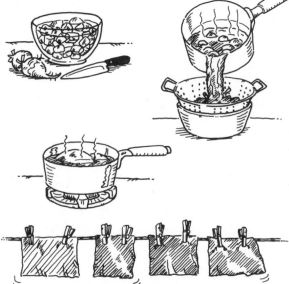

Plant	Color
Onion skins	yellow
Goldenrod flowers	yellow
Carrots	yellow
Red onions	pink
Raspberries	pink
Beets	rose
Coffee	brown
Nut hulls (not shells)	brown
Grass	green
Spinach	green

CARROT BASKET

123

Make a hanging carrot basket that would make any rabbit jealous.

cut

What You'll Need: Large carrot (at least two inches across) or parsnip, apple corer, toothpick, string, potting soil, grass seed

If you use a carrot for this project, find one of the novelty types that is at least two inches in diameter and still has its top. If you can't find one, use a parsnip or other thick root vegetable with the top still on.

Cut off the bottom of your vegetable, leaving the top three inches with the leaves. Next cut off the foliage, leaving about two inches of leafy stem. Use an apple corer to hollow out the vegetable top. (Turned upside-down, the vegetable top makes a basket.)With toothpicks, poke four evenly spaced holes around the cut edge of the basket. Cut four pieces of string about two feet long and tie one in each of the holes. Tie the strings together at the top. Fill the basket with potting soil and plant grass seed on top. Hang your basket up. If you keep the soil moist, it will sprout grass on top, while the vegetable tops will grow again, curling around the basket as they reach up for the sun. If you want, you can plant alfalfa seeds or the seeds of small flowers in your basket.

GROW CARROTS

124

Carrots are fun to grow—and even more fun to eat!

What You'll Need: Carrots, knife, flat dishes or deep saucers, gravel, water, potting soil

Start with carrots that have leafy tops. Cut off the tops leaving about two inches of greens. Cut off the top inch of the carrot, and plant it in potting soil or fine pebbles in a dish. Leave the greens above the surface. Keep the soil barely moist. If using pebbles, add fresh water every other day. When the carrots begin to sprout new leaves, plant in soil in a flower pot.

125 BEAN TENT

Grow a summer playhouse in your garden.

What You'll Need: Garden space, bean seeds, poles at least six feet long, string

Start with a sunny patch of garden space about four or five feet wide. Rake the soil smooth, then mark a circle with a diameter of about three or four feet. With help from an adult, stick poles into the soil all around the circle, about a foot apart, and tie them together at the top.

Tie a string to the base of one of the poles. Run the string around all the poles, looping it once or twice around each one. Leave a space between two poles as your doorway. Then run more string from the top of the poles to the string at the bottom, leaving about four or six inches of space between the strings. Plant your bean seeds all around the circle. Water them well after planting. Then water twice a week or as needed while the beans grow. Help the young bean plants find your tent poles and strings so they can grow up them. Soon you will have a shady tent to play in.

SUN-DRIED TOMATOES 126

These tomatoes are easy to make as a gift for gourmets.

What You'll Need: Tomatoes from garden or U-pick farm (plum tomatoes are best), knife, spoon, cookie sheets, oven, red wine vinegar, jars with lids, olive oil, plastic wrap

For this project, use only fresh, fully ripe tomatoes without any bruises. Have an adult help you with all cutting and cooking.

Cut the tomatoes in half and use a spoon to scoop out the seeds. Large tomatoes should be cut into quarters. Spread the tomatoes evenly on a cookie sheet. Put in an oven set to 150°F and dry until most of the moisture is gone but the tomatoes are still soft. Next, put the tomatoes in a bowl and sprinkle with red wine vinegar, then cover the bowl and allow to sit for at least 15 minutes. The vinegar helps preserve the tomatoes, and adds flavor. Pack the dried tomatoes loosely into a jar and pour in olive oil until completely covered. Cover the top of the jar with plastic wrap, then put on the lid. Store in the refrigerator.

PUMPKIN TUNNEL

127

Rediscover pumpkins: They aren't just for Halloween.

What You'll Need: Garden space, heavy concrete reinforcement mesh, or 11 poles about five feet long, pumpkin seeds

To build your tunnel, you'll need a sunny area of the garden about five feet wide. Have an adult cut a piece of mesh five feet wide and about six feet long. Shape it into an arch, pushing the ends of the wire on the five-foot long sides into the soil. Plant pumpkin, gourd, or cucumber seeds along the sides, or use transplants. As the plants grow, they will cover the mesh and make a nice tunnel to play in.

If concrete mesh is hard to find, you can make your tunnel from poles. Stick five poles in the ground one foot apart, then make another line of poles three feet away. Tie the tops to a cross pole to form the shape of a tunnel. Plant your seeds at the base of each pole. As the plants grow, you may want to tie them to the poles with strips of rag to help them climb.

Cover the floor of your tunnel with grass clippings or straw for comfort.

IT'S PLANTING TIME!

128

Different vegetables have different growing seasons.

What You'll Need: Gardening book, poster board, markers

Find out what vegetables grow in your area, and what time of year each vegetable should be planted. (Check the library for books and magazines on vegetable gardening, or ask a gardener or farmer you know.) Then make a chart that shows each vegetable, when to plant it, and when to harvest it. Your chart could also give other information, such as how much to water to give it and what pests to watch out for. You can use the poster to grow your own vegetables, or give it to someone who likes to garden.

129

SPORE PRINTS

Did you know that mushooms can make their own prints?

What You'll Need: Mushroom caps, white unlined index cards, black paper, drinking glass or bowl, hair spray or acrylic fixative

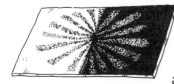

Find a mushroom in the wild, or get some from the store. (Be careful when handling wild mushrooms—don't eat them!) You will have to find some with the caps open. Look underneath the cap. The gills inside are lined with structures that make and release spores by the millions. Each spore can grow into a new fungus.

Cover half of an index card with black paper. Pop out the stem from the mushroom cap and place the cap on the card so that half is on the black paper and half on the white. Cover with a glass or bowl and let the cap sit overnight. The next day remove the glass and the mushroom cap. You should see a print of the mushroom spores. Pale spores will show up on the black paper, while darker ones will show on the white. Ask an adult to spray the print with hair spray or acrylic fixative to keep it from smearing.

SUGAR, SUGAR

130

Sugar cane is the perfect remedy for a sweet tooth.

What You'll Need: Sugar cane, potting soil, large flower pot (about eight inches), knife, candle

Most people don't know that sugar cane is a type of grass. Like grass, it grows quickly and easily into an attractive plant. Find a fresh-cut section of sugar cane at least a foot long. (You may have to look in a specialty grocery store.) Look near the joints in the stem for a shield-shaped bud from which new stalks will grow. Below the buds are tiny holes where roots will grow. Ask an adult to cut the stalk off two inches below the bud and about an inch above the next joint.

Fill a flower pot with potting soil up to about two inches from the rim. Stick the cane into the soil so that the bud is just barely covered. Have an adult help you light the candle and drip melted wax onto the other end of the cane to keep it from drying out. Keep the soil barely moist. In a week or two the bud will sprout. When the new sprout is about six inches high, add another 1½ inches of potting soil.

As more sprouts grow you can cut the sprouts, peel them, and cut them into sticks to stir hot drinks with.

A KITCHEN GARDEN

131

Look in your kitchen to find all sorts of fun things to grow!

What You'll Need: Fruit seeds (lemons, oranges, kiwis, grapes), potting soil, flower pots

Nearly any ripe seed will grow into a new plant. Collect seeds from fruits such as lemons and other citrus fruits or grapes. Then fill some flower pots with potting soil up to ½ inch from the top. Plant your seeds and watch them grow. Here are some special instructions for each:

Citrus fruits: Don't allow the seeds to dry out at all. Plant them right away in a mix of three parts potting soil and one part sand. Keep them well-watered—but not soggy. These plants like a lot of light.

Grapes: Grape seeds usually sprout easily. Keep them in a sunny window, and give the plant something to climb on.

Kiwi: Collect these tiny seeds with a toothpick and place them on a moist paper towel. Roll up the towel, put it in a plastic bag, and place it in the refrigerator for two weeks. Kiwi seeds need a cold period before they sprout. Plant on top of moist potting soil and cover with plastic wrap until the plants sprout. Be sure to give the young plants something to climb on.

GROW A PIZZA

132

When you're hungry for pizza, you can get one without ordering out.

What You'll Need: Plants that grow pizza ingredients (tomatoes, green peppers, onions, herbs), garden plot or large pots

Of course, growing your own pizza takes a little longer than having it delivered, but it can be worth the wait. What veggies do you like on your pizza? Grow them from seeds or seedlings starting in the spring, and plan a home-grown pizza party sometime in the summer. In addition to tomatoes, green peppers, and other pizza veggies, you can grow herbs for your pizza. Basil and oregano are the most commonly used. You might also try chives, rosemary, or other herbs. They're all easy to grow in small pots or in a garden.

When your pizza garden is ready all you'll need is a pizza crust, some cheese, and a few hungry friends.

WHAT A DOLL!

133

Corn husk dolls were made by Native Americans in what is now the northeastern United States. Here's how you can make one.

What You'll Need: Corn husks, string, scissors, markers, dried flowers (optional)

Strip the husks from several ears of corn. Let them dry out for a few days. Keep some of the corn silk to use for hair.

First, make the doll's head by rolling up one husk. Put some corn silk on top of the roll. Then put another corn husk over the silk and the rolled-up husk. Use string to tie this piece tightly under the rolled-up husk. This will be the face and neck.

Roll a husk lengthwise to make the arms. Tie the long roll at each end. Put this roll under the neck, and tie it in place.

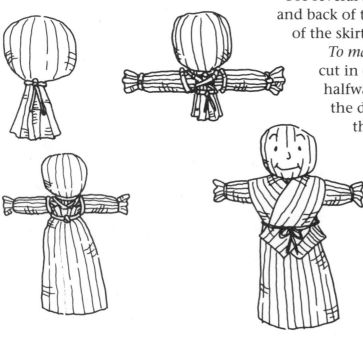

Use several husks to make a skirt. Lay these husks in the front and back of the arms, and tie them in place. Trim the bottom of the skirt so it is even.

To make a blouse: Cut a rectangle out of a husk. Make a cut in one end of the rectangle. The cut should go about halfway through the rectangle. Put the rectangle behind the doll, with the cut end up. The end of the rectangle that is not cut will be the back of the blouse. Fold the cut end of the rectangle over to the front of the doll. This will be the front of the blouse. Cross the two flaps over each other and use string to tie the blouse in place.

Finally, draw a face on your corn husk doll. You can put dried flowers in its hand or make a bonnet for its head out of corn husks, too!

BOX GARDEN

134

Turn a wooden fruit crate into a miniature salad garden.

What You'll Need: Wooden fruit crate, newspaper, potting soil, garden soil or compost, water, vegetable seeds (leaf lettuce, ball carrots, radishes, and miniature bush tomatoes)

In the winter, fruit shipped from places like South America often comes in wooden crates. Ask your grocer to save one for you. Line the crate with four or five layers of newspaper. Fill with a mixture of half potting soil and half garden soil or compost. Water the soil and allow the box to drain. Make two long furrows the length of the box, one near the front, the other right down the middle. Divide the front row in half. In one half sprinkle seeds for miniature carrots. In the other half sprinkle radish seeds. In the middle row, sprinkle leaf lettuce seeds. Plant the seeds thinly.

The back half of the box is for your bush tomatoes. Poke a hole about one-half inch deep and drop two or three tomato seeds in it. Cover the seeds. When they sprout wait until they are about two inches tall, then cut away the weaker plants, leaving one strong one.

Keep the box outside in a sunny place and water it every day. Thin the plants if they need it. Pull the carrots when they are about one inch across. Cut the lettuce when the leaves are about 6 to 8 inches tall.

SHOUT ABOUT SPROUTS

135

It's easy and fun to grow tasty sprouts for salads and sandwiches.

What You'll Need: Alfalfa seeds, quart jar, cheesecloth, rubber band, teaspoon

Wash and dry the jar. Measure two teaspoons of alfalfa seeds into the jar. Fill the jar half-full of water. Cover the top with three layers of cheesecloth, holding the layers in place with a rubber band. Swirl the jar around to rinse all the seeds, and pour the water out through the cheesecloth.

Place the jar in a warm, dry place, like a cupboard. The seeds should begin to sprout in a day or two. Each day, take the jar out, add more water, swirl to rinse the seeds, and pour the water out through the cheesecloth. When the sprouts are about two inches long, place the jar in a sunny window for a few days to green up. Keep rinsing the sprouts every day. After the sprouts have greened, put them in the refrigerator.

DREAM WEAVER

136

Create unique wall hangings from natural materials.

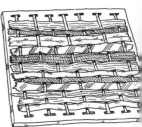

What You'll Need: Sturdy cardboard, scissors, string, wild plant material for weaving (dried grass, strips of bark peeled from twigs, etc.), craft glue

First you'll need to create your loom. Take a piece of cardboard just a little larger than the size of the weaving you want to make. Cut a row of slits in the top and bottom ends, making each slit ¼ to ½ inch apart. Tie a knot in your string, slip the knot into one of the slits to anchor it, then run the string to the slit on the opposite side. Slip the string behind the cardboard to the next slit on the same side, bring it through, then run it across the board again. Keep going until the whole piece of cardboard is strung, like strings on a guitar.

Now collect any kind of natural materials that are long and narrow, such as tall dried grass, strips of dried corn husk or cattail leaves, bark peeled from fallen twigs, or long pine needles. Weave these materials in and out of the strings in any way that pleases you. When your weaving is done, slip the ends of the string off the cardboard. Turn your weaving over and glue the edges to keep the weaving together.

WEAVING CATTAILS

137

Here's one way early Native Americans made mats from cattail's leaves.

What You'll Need: Cattails, bricks, sewing machine, quilting thread

The method used here will make a small sturdy mat, useful for hot dishes, for place mats, or for sitting on outdoors. Cattails can be found growing in many wet areas all over the country (and are also available in crafts stores). Just be sure you get permission from the land owner to gather them. Cut the leaves from the cattails and spread them out in a sunny place to dry completely. When dry, soak them a few minutes in water. Lay leaves out side by side until you have enough to form a square. Weigh the ends down on one side with bricks. Weave the remaining leaves over and under the leaves you laid out. When you are finished weaving, weigh the other ends of the leaves down with bricks and let the leaves dry.

To finish the edges, have an adult sew them together on a sewing machine using a heavy needle and sturdy quilting thread. If you can't find cattails, try other plants with long leaves, such as daylilies.

CORN HUSK MATS

138

These mats are just as useful now as they were to the pioneers who made them years ago.

What You'll Need: Corn husks, darning needle, quilting thread, thimble

Dry the corn husks outdoors in a sunny place until completely dry. When you are ready to use them, tear them into strips and soak the strips for an hour in warm water. Tie six strips together at one end and braid them together, using two strips in each "strand." When you have braided about two-thirds of the way down, add two more strips to each strand and keep going. The braid will hold together if your strips overlap one another sufficiently.

When your braid is long enough, tie off the end. Lay it down on a flat surface and begin coiling the braid around one of the end knots. As you coil, stitch the braids together with quilting thread. Use a strong darning needle and protect your finger with a thimble. Make small mats for coasters, or large ones to put under hot dishes on the dinner table.

THE HISTORY OF HERBS

People have used herbs for centuries. We sprinkle herbs in our soups and stews and sauces to make them taste better, and people throughout history have used certain herbs as medicines. Some thought that herbs had magic powers. Even today, many people believe that a four leaf clover can bring its finder good luck, and others use parsley as a symbol of victory.

APPLEHEAD DOLLS

139

These charming, old-fashioned dolls—made from small apples—look like wise old men and women.

What You'll Need: Small green apples, peeler, knife, wire, fabric scraps

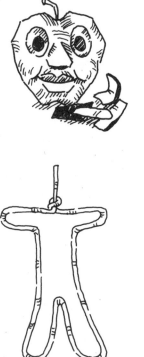

Begin with small, firm apples. Green, unripe apples work the best, so if you know someone with an apple tree you can ask them for some windfallen green apples. Peel the apple, then have an adult help you carve the face with a small knife. Think of how a real face is shaped. The nose and cheeks must stick out, while the eyes are set in, so carve away the front of the apple but leave lumps sticking out for the nose and cheeks. Make exaggerated features, as they will shrink in the drying process. Put the apple in a warm place to dry. This will take a week or more.

When the apple head is dry, bend wire into the shape of a body, with a long neck to stick into the apple head. Dress the doll with clothing cut from fabric scraps.

MEXICAN JUMPING BEANS

Frogs and rabbits can jump, but have you ever heard of a "jumping bean"? This type of Mexican bean seed has a small caterpillar living inside of it. When the caterpillar moves, the bean has to move, too. This jumping can last for several months until the caterpillar finally emerges from the bean as a small moth!

APPLE RINGS

140

This garland made from dried apples is a nice decoration that will make your house smell wonderful.

What You'll Need: Apples, apple corer, knife, twine

Have an adult help you core and slice several red-skinned apples. String the apple slices on a piece of twine. Make your garland as long as you like. When you're done, hang the garland up in your kitchen. In dry weather, the apples will slowly dry out and fill the kitchen with a fresh scent.

DRIED FRUIT TREATS

141

Turn this summer's harvest into tasty winter treats.

What You'll Need: Fruit, cookie sheets, nuts, meat grinder, lemon juice, coconut, plastic wrap, glass jar (optional)

Begin with some fresh, ripe fruit without bruises. With adult supervision, peel and slice larger fruits, removing seeds or pits. Slices should be about ¼ inch thick. Small berries can be dried whole, but bigger berries (such as strawberries) should be sliced. You can also buy bananas when they are inexpensive, slice them, and dry them.

To dry fruit: Spread the slices in a single layer on a cookie sheet. Put in an oven set to 150°F and dry until most of the moisture is gone but the fruit is still soft. Since you aren't using preservatives, the fruit will be brown. Pack into a jar and allow to sit a week or so before using. Eat your fruit as it is, or make fruit treats.

To make fruit treats: Measure out about two cups of dried fruit and one cup of nuts. Use a meat grinder to chop up the nuts and fruits finely. Moisten with about a tablespoon of lemon juice. Shape into small balls or logs. Roll in shredded coconut. Wrap each treat in plastic wrap. Pack into a pretty jar for a gift.

MAKE BERRY JAM

Jazz up your peanut butter with this tasty jam that you can make from fresh berries.

What You'll Need: Small bowl or plate, several jars with lids, two pounds of fresh berries that are just slightly underripe, four teaspoons of fresh lemon juice, large pot, wooden spoon, 1½ pounds of granulated sugar

If wild berries grow where you live, you can pick them and make them into jam. Or get your berries at a pick-them-yourself farm or roadside stand. Here's how to make jam from strawberries, blackberries, raspberries, or blueberries:

First, put a small bowl or plate in the refrigerator to chill. Next, put the jars that will hold the jam into the dishwasher, and run the dishwasher through a full cycle, including hot dry. The jars should still be warm when you're ready to pour in the jam.

Put two pounds of clean berries and four teaspoons of fresh-squeezed lemon juice in a very large pot or kettle. (Jam will froth and expand while it's cooking, so make sure there's plenty of extra room in the pot.) The berries should be just a little underripe, because ripe berries will make runny jam.

Use a big wooden spoon to squash the berries a little so that some of the juice is squeezed out. With adult supervision, cook the berries over low heat, stirring them all the time. Let the berries come to a boil. (Turn up the heat a little if you need to.) As soon as they are boiling, lower the heat and simmer the berries for five minutes. Don't forget to keep stirring!

Add the sugar gradually until it is all dissolved. Then turn the heat all the way up to high and boil the jam for at least 5 minutes. (How long it takes depends on what kind of berries you have and how ripe they are.) The mixture will be foamy. Remember to keep stirring and watch the jam closely so it doesn't boil over.

After about five minutes, test the jam to see if it is done. To do this, use the wooden spoon to place a few drops of jam onto the bowl that you have chilled. Put the bowl back in the fridge so the jam will cool. If the jam forms a "skin" that holds together when you touch it, it's ready. If not, cook the jam for another five minutes, then test it again.

When the jam is ready, pour it into the clean, warm jars. Seal the jars. When they're cool, label them and store in the refrigerator.

A BERRY NICE INK

143

Your friends will be surprised when you write them a secret note using special ink made from fresh berries.

What You'll Need: Berries, strainer, jar, spoon, vinegar, salt, smock

Wear a smock to protect your clothes from stains. Put one cup of ripe raspberries, blackberries, or blueberries into a strainer. Put the strainer over a large jar. Use the back of a spoon to crush the berries so their juice falls into the jar. Squeeze as much juice out of the berries as you can.

Add to the jar one teaspoon of vinegar and one teaspoon of salt, and stir until the salt is dissolved. Use your berry ink right away, because it will spoil quickly.

A TOMATO-BERRY?

Berries are an important food, but they are also far more widespread than is commonly thought. Plants that produce berries include grapes, blueberries, currants, tomatoes, bananas, eggplants, and dates. There are other foods that are closely related to the berry family, as well. Pumpkins, squashes, and cucumbers are pepos, which are a special kind of berry. Oranges, lemons, and grapefruits are another type of berry.

NATURE'S BEAUTY

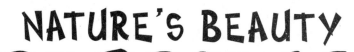

144

Be the apple of someone's eye with this apple centerpiece.

What You'll Need: Styrofoam cone, apples, greenery, plate, toothpicks

Buy a Styrofoam cone with a flat top at a crafts store. If your cone has a pointed top, cut off the point. Place the Styrofoam cone on a plate. Gather plenty of shiny red apples and some greenery, such as apple leaves or evergreen boughs.

Push a toothpick halfway into each apple. Then attach the apples to the Styrofoam cone by pushing the toothpicks into the cone. Start by making a row of apples around the bottom of the cone, with the apples resting on the plate. Then make another row right on top of that, and work your way to the top. It will work best if you put the bigger apples on the bottom, and the smaller ones on top. The last apple should go right on top of the cone.

Use the greenery to fill the spaces between the apples. You should be able to stick the ends of the leaves or boughs right into the cone. Finally, decorate the edges of the plate with greenery, too.

You can also make the centerpiece out of other fruits, such as oranges or lemons.

THE CAT'S MEOW

145

Cats go crazy for catnip, whether it's still growing or made into a toy.

What You'll Need: Felt, scissors, pen, needle, thread, catnip

Catnip is an herb that you can buy at a plant nursery and grow in a pot or garden. Cats love to play in it and eat it. Plant some catnip in a place where a cat can enjoy it.

Cut a piece of felt into an interesting shape, such as a mouse! Lay the shape on another piece of felt and trace around it. Cut out your tracing to make a second shape that's exactly the same as the first. With help from an adult, use a needle and thread to sew the two pieces of felt together, but leave a small opening. Stuff the toy with catnip, then sew it shut.

FRUIT LEATHER

146

Cook up some fruit rolls that are as much fun to make as they are to eat!

What You'll Need: Fruit (such as plums, peaches, and apricots), peeler, knife, measuring cup, sugar, water, saucepan, plastic wrap, cookie sheets, oven

You can make your own fruit rolls! Be sure to have an adult help you with this project. Peel fresh fruit, cut it up into small pieces, and put it in a measuring cup. For every quart of fruit, add one half cup of sugar and a half cup of water. Put the mixture into a saucepan and simmer on the stove until the fruit is soft and can be mashed up. Watch carefully to prevent scorching, and add more water as needed. Pour the cooked fruit into a blender and blend it into a thick puree.

Next, cut large squares of plastic wrap and lay them out on cookie sheets. Pour about ¼ to ½ cup of fruit puree onto each square and spread it out into a thin layer. Put the cookie sheets in an oven heated to no more than 150°F, leaving the oven door slightly open. Allow the puree to dry until leathery. Don't overheat the oven or over-dry the leather, or else it will turn crisp!

When the leather is done, roll it up in its plastic wrap and store in a jar. Peel it from the plastic wrap when you're ready to eat it. Yum! Plums, apricots, and peaches seem to make the best homemade leather, but you can experiment with other fruits as well.

NATURE'S NOISEMAKER

147

It's easy to make a grass whistle. All you need is one blade of green grass, and two thumbs.

Put your thumbs together, and hold the blade of grass between them. Blow into the crack between your thumbs, so the air flows over the grass. You should hear a whistling sound. If you don't hear anything, move the blade of grass a little, and try again. You'll soon get the hang of it.

VENUS FLYTRAPS

148

Carnivorous plants can be easy and fun to raise if you give them the right environment.

What You'll Need: Small aquarium or fish bowl or 1 gallon glass jar (or bottle terrarium—see page 220), peat moss, charcoal (use the kind prepared for house plants), potting soil, sand, old mixing bowl, water, Venus Flytrap plant, insects or tiny bits of raw meat

Pour a one-inch layer of crushed charcoal into the bottom of the terrarium. Mix three parts of potting soil with one part sand and one part peat moss in an old mixing bowl. Add water until the mix is moist but not soggy. Put about three inches of the mix into the terrarium. Now dig a small hole for your plant. Carefully remove the Venus fly-trap from its pot and plant it in the hole. Put a cover on the terrarium. You need to keep your plant moist. Most purchased Venus Flytrap plants die because of improper care. The air in your living room is too dry for them. Venus Flytraps are bog plants, so they need humid air and wet soil to survive.

The Venus Flytrap eats insects because it needs nutrients, since bog soils are low in nutrients. You can feed your plant small insects or tiny bits of raw meat. Put a bit of meat on a leaf and gently tap it to make the leaf close. Be aware that Venus Flytraps are becoming rare because of over collection. Many are collected illegally. When you buy yours, check the label to see if it is greenhouse raised or collected from the wild. Be sure to only purchase greenhouse raised plants.

WHAT IS "SYMBIOSIS"?

Plants and animals often rely on each other for survival. This is called "symbiosis." On the island of Mauritius, there used to be a tree called the tambalacoque. A huge, flightless bird called the dodo used to eat the seeds of that tree, and the digestive system of the dodo bird would crack the seeds open, so they could sprout. Eventually, the dodo bird died out, however, and the tambalacoque tree died along with it. Apparently, after the dodo died, no other species of bird could crack open the hard shell of the tambalacoque.

SURVIVING IN THE DESERT

149

Have you ever wondered how desert plants live on very little water?

What You'll Need: Paper towels, water, cookie sheet, paper clips, waxed paper

Wet three paper towels until they are saturated with water but not dripping. Put one of the paper towels flat on a cookie sheet. Roll up the second paper towel, paper clip it to keep it rolled up, and put it on the cookie sheet, too. Put the third paper towel on a piece of waxed paper that is the same size. Roll up the waxed paper and the paper towel together, and paper clip them so they stay rolled up.

Leave all three paper towels where they are for 24 hours. Then check them. The flat one will be dry. The rolled one will be dry or mostly dry. But the paper towel that is rolled up with the waxed paper will still be wet.

Now, you may be asking, "What does this have to do with plants in the desert?" Here's the answer: Cacti and other desert plants are like the paper towel that is rolled up with waxed paper. These plants have waxy coverings that keep moisture from evaporating into the dry desert air. That's part of the reason they can survive on the little water they get in the desert.

PLANT SUCCESSION

150

From weeds to trees, here's how Mother Nature takes back her land.

What You'll Need: A field that is in transition, notebook, pen

If you have a lawn, you know that somebody has to mow it all summer long. (Maybe it's you!) Did you ever wonder what would happen if the lawn didn't get mowed? Other plants might start growing in and around the grass. After that, small bushes and shrubs would begin to grow. If you live in an area where there are woods, trees would eventually grow.

This process is called plant succession. In some areas, you can see plant succession happening in nature. Look for land that was once farmland or pasture that has been abandoned. Once you've found a piece of land to study, check on it several times throughout the year. Keep a journal and take notes on the land's progress. Nature will gradually reclaim this land, covering it with native plants, shrubs, and trees.

THIS GARDEN ROCKS!

151

If you're a rock lover, it's fun to make a garden that features rocks, as well as plants.

What You'll Need: Garden plot, rocks of different shapes and sizes, plants

If you have a yard or garden area that already has some large rocks in it, you're in luck. If not, gather some rocks when you go out hiking. (A wagon or wheelbarrow comes in very handy!)

Begin arranging the rocks in your garden space. You may want to draw a plan of your rock garden first. It's a lot easier to move rocks around on paper than in the garden! Arrange the rocks in a design you like. It's nice to have one place in a garden that is the main attraction. If you have a favorite rock, put it in a place where it will be the "star" of the garden. Use more rocks to make a border around the garden, if you like.

Of course, you'll want plants in your garden, too. For ideas, here is a list of flowering plants that are popular in rock gardens. But which plants you choose will depend on where you live and what kinds of plants you like. Your rock garden could also be an herb garden! Or, you could plant different kinds of plants that all have the same color flowers. If you live where it's warm and dry, your rock garden could be a cactus garden, with many kinds of cactus.

Popular Rock Garden Plants	
Alyssum	Geranium
Anemone	Iris
Azalea	Narcissus
Crocus	Phlox
Cyclamen	Rhododendron

GARDEN MARKERS

152

These attractive painted signs will make nice presents for any gardeners on your gift list.

What You'll Need: Seed packets or catalogs, markers, thin scrap wood, coping saw, acrylic paint, spray varnish, small nails, small stakes

Some people like to mark their garden rows with stakes and stick the empty seed packet on top of the stake. Painted garden markers are a much prettier way to show what you've planted.

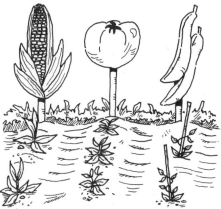

Use pictures from seed packets or catalogs to help you draw four- to six-inch-wide pictures of the vegetables your family likes to plant in the garden. Trace the outline of each picture onto thin scrap wood and have an adult cut the shapes out with a coping saw. With your drawings and the pictures to guide you, paint in the shapes with acrylic paints. Let the paint dry. Ask an adult to help you cover with three coats of spray varnish, allowing the varnish to dry between coats. Be sure to work in a well ventilated area and use a type of varnish that is suitable for the outdoors. Carefully nail the painted shapes to garden stakes about two feet long.

MAP YOUR YARD

153

How well do you think you know your yard? Find out when you draw a nature map.

What You'll Need: Large piece of paper, markers, field guide to plants and trees

First, try to draw a map of your yard from memory. No peeking outside! How much can you remember? When you're finished, take a look and compare, then make another yard map that shows how much you know about nature. Map all the trees, shrubs, flowers, and so on. Label them with their names. Also include any other interesting features of your yard, such as large rocks and animal homes.

A VISUAL "DIARY"

154

You'll remember your next nature trip long after it's over when you create this "natural wonders" wall hanging.

What You'll Need: Small objects from nature, jute twine, four sticks or twigs, craft glue, wire or small hooks

When you go on a nature hike, collect small objects such as twigs, grasses, flowers, nuts, bark, and shells. When you get home, you can weave all the objects together to make an artistic record of your trip.

First, make a frame for your artwork. Tie together four twigs or sticks to make a square or rectangle. Next wrap natural jute twine around the frame. Use the twine as a base on which to mount all the other objects. You can weave them through the twine, use small hooks or pieces of wire to hook them on, or glue them on. You could attach the objects to the frame in the order you found them or in an artistic design. Either way, you'll have a unique "diary" of your trip.

WHAT TRANSPIRED?

155

Plants transpire, which means their leaves give off water vapor. Try this experiment to gather up the water that a leaf transpires.

What You'll Need: Potted plant, plastic bag, tape

You can't see a plant transpiring. But here's a way to prove it's happening:
Tape a plastic bag tightly around one stem of a plant. Observe the bag each day for a week. Be sure to water the plant. What happens? What do you think is the source of the moisture you see in the bag? It comes from the leaves through tiny pores on the underside.

GOING IN CIRCLES

156

Make your own wreath for Christmas—or any other time of year—using materials you find in nature.

What You'll Need: Vines, decorations (leaves, dried flowers)

To make the basic wreath, you'll need several vines. You can find grapevines or honeysuckle vines in nature. Collect them in the winter when they are dormant. If the vines are too dry and brittle to bend, soak them in water until they are more flexible. Bend the vines into a circle. Weave several circles of vine together to make your wreath. Wrap small vines around the wreath to help hold it together.

You can leave your vine wreath plain or decorate it any way you like. For the fall, you could add grape leaves and clusters of grapes to your wreath. (Real grapes won't last very long. You can use artificial grapes or even make your own from clay or paper.) Or decorate your wreath with dried flowers or evergreen and winter berries.

PRICKLY PETS

157

Those big, prickly burrs from burdock plants can be a pain in the neck—or the foot! Here's how you can change them into cute burr babies.

What You'll Need: Dried burrs from burdock plants, craft glue, twigs, maple wings (optional), paint

Burrs can also be a big pain in the paw for your four-footed friends. So, pick them up off the ground and use them for this great craft. Glue several burrs together to make animal shapes. Add tiny twigs for legs, maple wings (they carry the seeds of maple trees) for wings, and other natural decorations to finish them off. You can use tiny dabs of paint to give them eyes. Make a whole zoo of burr babies, and keep them up on a shelf, where they won't bite any toes!

BE A NATURE ARTIST

158

Try your hand at making some botanical drawings that can be framed or made into greeting cards.

What You'll Need: Drawing paper or a sketch pad, colored pencils or markers

"Botanical" means "having to do with the science of plants." Botanical drawings are drawings of plants that are both beautiful and scientific. They show all the different parts of the plant, as close to the way they really look as possible. See if you can find some examples of botanical drawings at your library, then create your own.

You may want to draw your own creations in a spiral-bound sketch pad, and keep adding to your collection. Colored pencils are good to use for botanical drawings, because you can make very exact drawings with them. Start by drawing a simple plant. Label the different parts of the plant (stem, leaves, flower, etc.).

Another way to make botanical drawings is to show a plant at different times of the year. For example, you could make four drawings of a tree, showing how it looks in spring, summer, fall, and winter.

"LOOK MOM, NO DIRT!"

159

Believe it or not, while most plants in nature grow in soil, it's possible to grow plants without it.

What You'll Need: Wire mesh, aquarium, plant food, water, sphagnum moss, bean or corn seeds

Put a piece of wire mesh (like a piece of old screen) in the bottom of an empty aquarium. Bend the ends of the mesh so that it makes a shelf that is several inches above the bottom of the aquarium. Mix plant food into some water, and pour the water into the aquarium. The water level should be just below the mesh. Put some sphagnum moss on top of the mesh. Then sprinkle some bean or corn seeds onto the moss, and water them well. Keep the seeds watered. Even though there's no soil, the seeds will sprout and send roots down through the mesh into the water that contains plant food.

ONE USEFUL PLANT

Much of your clothing is probably made out of cotton, which grows on a plant. It grows in the southern part of the country, since the cotton plant needs a long, sunny growing season. The hairlike fibers surrounding the seeds of the plant are used to make clothing. Other parts of the cotton plant are used as well, with cottonseed oil used to make soap and margarine.

160 PLANTASTIC PLANTS

The science and art of growing plants is called "horticulture." Read about it and maybe you'll grow a green thumb.

What You'll Need: One or more books about plants, pen, paper

There's a whole world of plants out there. At the library, find a book about plants, flowers, or gardening. See what you can learn. Then, do something with what you learned. You might plant your first garden, or grow just one flower.

Afterwards, write about the experience. Or, you might make a picture book showing the life cycle of a plant. Be sure to give the book a title and sign the author's name...yours!

FLOWER FUN

A flower garden can be anything from a half-acre plot to a flower pot. If you are fortunate, you might have a small plot of ground to call your own where you can plant anything you like. In this section, you'll learn how to have spring flowers in the winter, how to attract butterflies to your yard, and how to eat your roses! The chapter is full of activities to guide you in growing both indoor and outdoor flowers. And the flowers you grow can be used for some fun crafts and activities.

161

COLORFUL CARNATION

Do flowers ever get thirsty? In this project, you can actually watch a flower "drink" water.

What You'll Need: White carnation, scissors or knife, two glasses, water, red and blue food coloring

Get a white carnation with a long stem. With help from an adult, very carefully cut the carnation's stem lengthwise, from the bottom to about halfway up to the flower. Now fill two glasses with water. Use food coloring to color the water in one of the glasses dark red. Color the water in the other glass dark blue. Put the glasses right next to each other. Put one half of the carnation stem into each glass. Check the carnation a day later, and two days later. Can you tell that the carnation has been drinking the water? You'll notice that the water travels up the tubes into the stem to reach the other parts of the plant.

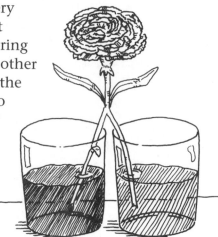

HERB/FLOWER NOSEGAYS

162

Can you crack the code? Discover how you and your friends can send secret messages—with flowers!

What You'll Need: Herbs and flowers, florist's tape (available from a crafts store)

Nosegays were small, scented bouquets that ladies of old carried when they went out walking, because the streets in the Middle Ages were smelly! Nosegays could also be used to pass secret messages, for people have given many flowers symbolic meanings.

Select a large flower to form the center of your nosegay, such as a daisy or a partially opened rose. Wrap the stem in florist's tape. Next, surround the center flower with a ring of flowers or herbs and wrap tightly with florist's tape. Keep adding layers until the nosegay is as big as you want it to be. Use ferns or large green leaves for the outer layer.

If you'd like to send a friend a floral message in a nosegay, here are what some flowers and herbs symbolize.

Alyssum	noble character
Apple blossom	beauty and goodness
Bracken fern	enchantment
Buttercup	radiance
Chamomile	courage
Carnation, pink	encouragement
Carnation, red	I must see you
Carnation, white	devotion
Cherry blossom	increase of friendship
Daisy	innocence
Fennel	strength
Forget-me-not	remembrance
Fuchsia	warning
Holly	good health
Juniper	protection
Lemon balm	sympathy
Marjoram	innocence, blushes
Mint	virtue, character, riches
Pansy	kind thoughts
Rose, white	purity
Rose, pink	love
Rosemary	remembrance
Strawberry leaves	perfection
Thyme	virtue, honesty
Zinnia	thoughts of absent friends

FLOWER BOTTLES

163

These wonderful little bottles make great gifts for anyone who likes dried flowers.

What You'll Need: Bottles or wide-mouth jars; dried, small flowers, seed pods, and seed heads; sand; plaster of Paris; long tweezers; cork

Collect bottles, such as salad dressing or vinegar bottles. (Keep in mind, little fingers may work better using wide-mouthed jars. If necessary, use peanut butter or canning jars instead.) Clean and dry the bottles and remove labels. You can also buy attractive bottles at a crafts store. Now collect and dry small flowers, seed pods, and seed heads. Keep the size of your bottles in mind as you collect your flowers. Dry your flowers, seed pods, and seed heads (see page 113). Cut the stems to different lengths to form a pleasing arrangement. Mix two parts clean sand with one part plaster of Paris. Add enough water to make a thick liquid. Pour one or two inches of the mixture into the bottle. Stick the stems inside the bottle into the sand mixture using the tweezers to help you. Allow the sand mixture to dry. Close the bottle with a cork.

You can also make small dried flower scenes by using low, wide jars instead of bottles. Add small figurines or polished rocks and decorate the lid of the jar.

NATURE'S PERFUME

164

Say, is that peppermint? Give your nose a treat by planting lovely scented geraniums

What You'll Need: Potted scented-leaf geranium plants

Many plants have flowers that smell good. But some plants have *leaves* that smell good. A good example is the scented geranium. Its scent can range from peppermint to lemon to nutmeg—even coconut! You can grow it in pots indoors, or outdoors in summer. Buy some small potted geraniums at a plant nursery. Be sure to tell the nursery worker that you want "scented" geraniums, because there are many varieties of geraniums that are not scented. Let your friends sniff them and guess the scents.

165 DRYING FLOWERS

Preserve the beauty of flowers. Even fragile types of flowers can be dried to enjoy for years.

What You'll Need: Fresh-cut flowers, sand, leak-proof box (such as a shoe box)

Cut the flowers early in the day, after the dew has dried. Pour a layer of sand into a box. Lay your flowers in the sand with at least an inch of space between them. Gently spoon more sand over the flowers, making sure it gets between petals, until the flowers are covered. If the box is deep enough, you can add another layer of flowers.

If the flowers are delicate, find a box deep enough for them to stand upright in. Pour a layer of sand on the bottom and stick the flower stems into it. Carefully pour more sand around the flowers until they are covered.

Leave the boxes alone for at least two weeks. At the end of that time, carefully pour out some of the sand and check your flowers for dryness. Larger flowers will take more time to dry than smaller ones.

A NATURAL NECKLACE 166

In Hawaii, people make flower necklaces called leis. You can make a dazzling flower necklace, too.

What You'll Need: Flowers with stems (such as daisies)

To make a necklace, first you'll need to pick a lot of wild flowers that have long stems, such as daisies. (Be careful if you use dandelions, because the same yellow color that rubs off on your hands or chin can get messy.) Here's how to chain them together:

Cross two stems at right angles. Loop the vertical stem around the horizontal one so it ends up alongside the horizontal stem. Next lay a third stem at right angles to the two horizontal stems. Loop it around both horizontal stems. Keep adding stems this way until your lei is as long as you want it. Tie the last stem to the first flower to make a circle. Aloha!

STOP AND EAT THE ROSES

167

Some flowers look good, smell good, AND taste good!

What You'll Need: Rose blooms, sugar syrup, pot, waxed paper

Grow or buy some organically grown roses. (Since you're going to eat them, you don't want the roses to have chemical fertilizer or pesticides on them.) When the roses bloom, pick some. Have an adult carefully dip them into boiling sugar syrup. Put them on waxed paper to cool. When they are cool enough to handle, spread out the petals and let the flowers dry in the sun or in a warm (not hot) oven. Then help yourself to rose candy.

There's another part of the rose plant that tastes good. In the late summer or early fall, roses form "rose-hips." When the rose hips turn red, they are ripe and ready to eat. Just remove the seeds. Rosehips have a lot of vitamin C. They can also be used to make tea.

ROSE PETAL JAM

168

Make this sweet, fragrant treat from the flower garden.

What You'll Need: Rose petals, scale, water, pot, sugar, lemon juice, jam jars

Gather some roses in the morning after the dew has dried. Try to pick all of one kind, or find scents that will blend well together. Pick off the petals and cut off the white ends, which tend to be bitter.

For every half pound of rose petals, add one cup of water. With help from an adult, simmer five minutes on the stove to soften the petals. Add 1¼ cups of sugar and three tablespoons of lemon juice. Bring to a boil, then simmer for about 30 minutes until the mixture is thick. To test the jam, pour a few drops from a spoon onto a cold saucer and allow the jam to cool. If it seems jellylike, the jam is ready. Take the pan off of the stove and allow it to cool for ten minutes.

Sterilize clean jam jars by pouring a half inch of boiling water into them. Allow it to steam a few minutes, then turn the jar upside down on a dish rack. Be sure to use a pot holder when handling hot jars! Now fill the hot jars with jam. Each half pound of rose petals will make about a pint of jam. Close the jars and keep the jam in the refrigerator.

ROSE BEADS

169

These lovely beads, which were popular in Victorian times for making necklaces and rosaries, will keep their scent for decades.

What You'll Need: Rose petals, food processor or blender, water or rose oil (optional), straight pins, corrugated cardboard, light fishing line or dental floss, needle

If someone in your family has some old rose beads, you know how long they stay sweet-smelling! These beads are easier than ever to make these days thanks to the modern food processor.

Pick the roses early in the morning before the sun drives off some of the scent. Choose roses with similar scents, or blend scents that go well together. Most colors will blend well, as the beads will all darken to a mahogany color.

Ask an adult to put one handful of petals in the food processor at a time and process them until you have a thick paste. You may add a few drops of water if needed, or even a bit of rose oil if you have it. If necessary, you can spoon the paste into a jar and keep it refrigerated while you wait for more roses to bloom.

When you have enough paste, roll it into pea-sized beads. Run a pin through each bead and stick the pin into a piece of cardboard. Let the beads dry thoroughly. String on light fishing line or dental floss.

NATURE'S FORECASTERS

Did you know that the petals of the scarlet pimpernel have been used to predict rain? In England, gardeners watch this flower closely. If the amount of water in the air climbs up to 80 percent, the petals of the scarlet pimpernel close up, probably to protect itself from the water. The gardeners then expect rain to fall.

FRUIT PEEL FLOWERS

170

Try making these unusual Victorian flower decorations.

What You'll Need: Peels from citrus fruits, spoon, scissors, cookie sheet, craft glue, candy box, black paper or cloth

Back in Victorian days, artificial flowers were often made from paper or feathers, but sometimes from the peels of oranges, lemons, and grapefruit. To make these flowers, first peel some oranges or other citrus fruits. Use the edge of a spoon to carefully scrape away the white part of the peel until you see fine lines close to the outer, colored part. Rinse and dry the peels; use scissors to cut into the shapes of flower petals and leaves. With help from an adult, spread them out on a cookie sheet and dry in a warm oven (no hotter than 150°F). Don't let them over-dry or they will be brittle. When the shapes are dry they will curl into natural petal shapes.

Next, line an empty candy box with black paper or cloth. Use strong glue to glue the petals into flower shapes on the black background. You can use small seeds from oranges or lemons for flower centers.

PLANT A RAINBOW

171

Here's how to make an earth-bound rainbow that's as colorful as a rainbow in the sky.

What You'll Need: Garden plot, seeds of annual plants and flowers (see below)

For your rainbow garden, use seeds of plants in all colors of the rainbow. You can plant different colors of the same plant, or a different plant for each color. You could even plant them in the shape of a rainbow! These flowers are all summer-blooming annuals that will bloom well in all climate zones:

Color	Plant
Red and pink	Dianthus, petunia, verbena, zinnia
Yellow and orange	Calendula, marigold, zinnia
Green	Choose any nonflowering, leafy green plant, such as mint
Blue and purple	Dianthus, petunia, verbena, zinnia

CANDIED VIOLETS

172

What's purple and sweet and looks great on a cake?

What You'll Need: Violet blossoms, cookie sheet, egg white, small paintbrush, granulated sugar

Candied violets make a very special decoration for cakes, cupcakes, or frosted cookies. Pick some violet flowers from violets you have grown yourself or violets growing wild. (If you pick wild violets, be sure they haven't been sprayed with pesticides or chemical fertilizers. Also, be very sure that the flowers you're picking are violets. Ask an experienced adult to look at them, to make sure. Not all pretty flowers are edible!) Lay the violet blossoms on a cookie sheet, and carefully paint them with egg white. Then sprinkle them with plenty of sugar. Bake them in the oven at 300°F for about 45 minutes. When cool, your candied violets will be ready to decorate pastries.

LATE BLOOMERS

173

Find flowers, berries, and leaves for a beautiful winter bouquet.

What You'll Need: Field guide to plants

Most people think flowers only grow in the spring and summer, but there are several hardy winter-blooming plants. For example, a flower called the Christmas rose blooms in December and stays colorful all the way to early spring. And as long as they get some sunlight, pansies and violas will bloom in cold climates. See if you can find some winter blooms in your neighborhood.

Also look for plants that make bright-colored berries in the winter. Depending on where you live, you might find the berry-bearing bushes listed here. All are evergreen, which means their leaves stay green in winter. The berries may be red, orange, yellow, purple, or white. (Never eat the berries. They may be poisonous.) Use a field guide to plants to help you identify more flowers and plants for your winter bouquet.

Winter Flowers	Winter Berries
Christmas rose (Helleborus)	Barberry (Berberis)
Erysimum	Euonymus
Pansy	Holly (Ilex)
Polyanthus	Nandina
Viola	Pyracantha

174 SUNFLOWER COOKIES

These yummy sunflower treats are great for all kinds of flower nuts!

What You'll Need: 1 package (20 ounces) refrigerated peanut butter cookie dough, ⅓ cup all-purpose flour, large bowl, wooden spoon, cookie sheet, chocolate frosting, ½ cup unsalted sunflower seeds, decorations: yellow and green icing

Preheat your oven to 375°F. Remove dough from wrapper according to package directions; place in a large bowl; add flour. Mix dough and flour well with a wooden spoon.

Divide dough in 8 equal sections; then, divide each section in half. Roll half a section of dough into a ball; flatten on cookie sheet to 2½-inch thickness. Roll other half into 5-inch long rope. Cut 2 inches from rope for stem. Cut remaining 3 inches into 10 equal sections; roll into small balls for petals. Repeat with remaining dough.

Assemble your cookies, then bake 10 to 11 minutes or until lightly browned. Cool 4 minutes on cookie sheets. Remove to wire racks; cool completely.

Spread chocolate frosting in the center of each cookie; sprinkle with sunflower seeds. Decorate petals with yellow icing and decorate stem with green icing. Makes 8 cookies.

EASTER LILIES 175

Grow these holiday favorites as gifts for your family and friends.

What You'll Need: Easter lily bulbs, 6-inch wide flower pots, potting soil

Pour about four inches of soil into each of your flower pots. Put an Easter lily bulb onto the soil, and fill in around it with more potting soil until the bulb is barely covered. Moisten the soil, then put the pot aside in a cool, dark place. After about two weeks the stalk will sprout from the bulb. Fill in with more soil. Keep adding soil as the stalk grows until you have filled the pot to within ½ inch of the top.

Two months after you have planted the bulbs, bring them into a well-lit room. Mist the leaves daily with a plant mister or spray bottle. In a cool room, the plant will take about three months to bloom. In a warm room, it may take two months or less.

TAME THE WILDFLOWERS!

176

They're called wildflowers, of course, because they grow wild. But you can also grow wildflowers in your garden.

What You'll Need: Wildflower seeds, a garden plot

Wildflowers are hardy plants that are used to growing and blooming without a lot of pampering. You may be able to buy wildflower seeds, or you can collect them in nature. (First check to see if there are laws in your area about harvesting wildflower seeds.) Here's how to do it: Pay attention to what wildflowers grow in your area. You'll often see them in parks and meadows and along roadsides. Of course, they're most noticeable when they're blooming. Different wildflowers bloom at different times, from spring through summer and into fall.

When you see a type of wildflower that you like, watch it closely. The seed heads of most wildflowers are ready to pick three or four weeks after they bloom. Use a small garden clipper to clip off the seed heads, including the stems. Put them in a small paper bag or envelope and store them at room temperature in a dry place. Only take a few seed heads in any area. That way, you'll leave plenty of seeds for nature to grow next year's wild crop. And, of course, if you're on private property, get permission first.

In most cases, you'll plant the seeds in late summer or early fall. Wildflowers like lots of sunlight. Plant them in broken up soil, and be sure the seeds are covered with soil. Otherwise, they'll become bird seed! Water the seeds well when you first plant them. If it doesn't rain, keep the seeds watered. The following spring, you'll have "tame" wildflowers.

WONDERFUL WILDFLOWERS

There are more than 15,000 different kinds of wildflowers found in the United States and Canada alone. Their unusual names include flower-of-an-hour, yellow false garlic, tufted loosestrife, and stinking Benjamin. Beyond those 15,000 wildflowers, there is a huge assortment of non-flowering wild plants, including interrupted ferns and silver moss.

STATELY FLOWERS

177

Each state has an official flower—a flower that grows in the state and is a symbol of the state. Grow your state's flower.

What You'll Need: Encyclopedia or almanac, pot and potting soil, seeds or seedling

Find out from the list on the right what your state flower is. Why do you think that flower was picked as a symbol of your state? What about other states? Do any states share the same flower? Does your town or county have its own official flower? You can grow your state flower, either from seeds or from a seedling you buy at a nursery. Or pick another state. Maybe you want to try to grow all the states!

Alabama	Camellia	**Montana**	Bitterroot
Alaska	Forget-me-not	**Nebraska**	Goldenrod
Arizona	Saguaro cactus blossom	**Nevada**	Sagebrush
Arkansas	Apple blossom	**New Hampshire**	Purple lilac
California	Golden poppy	**New Jersey**	Purple violet
Colorado	Rocky mountain columbine	**New Mexico**	Yucca
Connecticut	Mountain laurel	**New York**	Rose
Delaware	Peach blossom	**North Carolina**	Dogwood
District of Columbia	American beauty rose	**North Dakota**	Wild prairie rose
Florida	Orange blossom	**Ohio**	Scarlet carnation
Georgia	Cherokee rose	**Oklahoma**	Mistletoe
Hawaii	Yellow hibiscus	**Oregon**	Oregon grape
Idaho	Syringa	**Pennsylvania**	Mountain laurel
Illinois	Native violet	**Rhode Island**	Violet
Indiana	Peony	**South Carolina**	Yellow jessamine
Iowa	Wild rose	**South Dakota**	Pasqueflower
Kansas	Native sunflower	**Tennessee**	Iris
Kentucky	Goldenrod	**Texas**	Bluebonnet
Louisiana	Magnolia	**Utah**	Sego lily
Maine	White pine cone and tassel	**Vermont**	Red clover
Maryland	Black-eyed susan	**Virginia**	Dogwood
Massachusetts	Mayflower	**Washington**	Western rhododendron
Michigan	Apple blossom	**West Virginia**	Big rhododendron
Minnesota	Pink and white lady's-slipper	**Wisconsin**	Wood violet
Mississippi	Magnolia	**Wyoming**	Indian paintbrush
Missouri	Hawthorn		

MOONLIGHT BLOOMS

178

Most flowers bloom in daylight; a few special ones bloom only at night.

What You'll Need: Seeds or seedlings of night-blooming flowers (see below); a garden plot or pots, potting soil

Night-blooming plants are pollinated by night-flying moths, and they smell great. In late spring, plant some night-blooming flowers such as the ones listed below. Or ask at a plant nursery for the names of other night bloomers that grow in your area. You can grow the flowers from seeds or from seedlings. Plant them in the ground or in pots. Either way, plant them in a place where you'll be able to enjoy their sweet scents.

Evening primrose *(Oenothera biennis)*
Moonflower *(Ipomoea alba)*
Evening-scented stock *(Matthiola longipetala)*

Flowering tobacco *(Nicotiana)*
Thorn apple *(Datura)*

179

INVENT A FLOWER

There are lots of interesting flowers in nature. Try to create your own.

What You'll Need: Parts of flowers and plants (either real or in photographs), scissors, craft glue, poster board or cardboard

Can you guess just how big the world's biggest flowers are? Well, they're called rafflesia and they can be as much as three feet wide and weigh as much as 15 pounds. They have almost no leaves and no stems—they're all flower! You've probably never seen one, since they only grow in the rain forests of Indonesia. Other unusual flowers include the bee flower, which looks so much like a bee that real bees get confused. And there's actually a flower called the carrion flower ("carrion" means dead flesh) that looks and smells like dead meat.

What wild kinds of flowers can you come up with? Find out by inventing a flower. Gather parts of different flowers and plants: leaves, stems, flowers, seeds, etc. Or, cut out plant and flower parts from pictures in old magazines. Glue the parts together on a piece of cardboard or poster board to make a crazy new flower.

CHANGING COLORS

180

Hydrangea flowers can be blue or pink, depending on where they grow.

What You'll Need: Red cabbage, shredded; pitcher or jar; pot; water; strainer; drinking glass; baking soda; white vinegar

Put one cup of shredded red cabbage in a heat-proof pitcher or jar. With help from an adult, bring some water to a boil. Pour the boiling water over the cabbage and let it steep for at least five minutes. Then pour the liquid through a strainer to remove the cabbage. Throw the cabbage away.

Put a few teaspoons of liquid in a glass; it should be reddish-purple. Stir some baking soda into the glass, ⅛ teaspoon to start. Keep adding baking soda until the liquid turns green. Next, stir white vinegar into the glass, ½ teaspoon at a time. Keep adding vinegar until the liquid turns back to red.

Why did the liquid turn different colors? The solution with the baking soda is alkaline, and solution with the vinegar is acid. Plant pigments (colors) are affected by alkaline and acid substances. The alkali made the cabbage broth turn green; the acid made it turn back to red. Soil can vary in how acid or alkaline it is—just like the two liquids varied. A hydrangea growing in very alkaline soil produces greenish flowers. Can you guess what color the flowers are when the hydrangea is planted in acid soil?

CALLING ALL BUTTERFLIES

181

Plant a special garden that will attract all kinds of butterflies.

What You'll Need: Garden plot, seeds or seedlings of plants butterflies enjoy (see below)

There are more than 10,000 known species of butterfly in the world. Of course, there aren't that many in your neighborhood, but chances are good you can find quite a few different varieties. First go to a plant nursery and look for the plants listed below. The best time to plant a butterfly garden is in late spring or early summer. Try to find other plants that help attract butterflies in your area.

Milkweed, a favorite of Monarch butterflies
Butterfly bush (also called *Buddleia*)
Butterfly weed (also called *Asclepias tuberosa*)

VEGGIE FLOWERS

182

Did you know that some vegetables actually grow flowers?

What You'll Need: Root vegetables, garden plot (or some pots and potting mix with plenty of sand or vermiculite)

Plants such as potatoes, carrots, turnips, radishes, sweet potatoes, and beets are very talented; they produce vegetables one year, and flowers the next. Here's how to prove it:

Cut the bottom half off some of the root vegetables just mentioned. Push the top half of each vegetable into some potting mix in a garden or pot. (A potato prefers to grow in water. Put the potato in a jar of water. Half the potato should be underwater, and the potato should not be touching the bottom of the jar. Stick toothpicks in the potato to keep it from touching the bottom.) Keep the veggies well watered. Soon, they'll sprout stems and leaves. And after that, they'll blossom. Notice the different kinds of flowers produced by the different vegetables. What is your favorite kind of flowering vegetable?

BEAUTIFUL BULBS

183

Brighten your winter by growing fresh spring flowers—indoors!

What You'll Need: Narcissus or hyacinth bulbs, shallow dish, pebbles or aquarium gravel, water

Narcissus and hyacinth bulbs can be grown indoors using the technique called "forcing." To "force" a bulb, you trick it into thinking it's springtime.

Buy some Paper-white narcissus bulbs or any type of hyacinth bulb at a garden store. Find a dish about three or four inches deep and pour in about 1 or 1½ inches of pebbles. Set three or four bulbs upright in the dish and fill in around them with more pebbles. Leave the tops of the bulbs sticking out. Add water up to the top of the pebbles. Set the dish in a cool, dark place for two weeks, adding water as needed, to allow roots to form. After two weeks, bring the dish out into a well-lit room, but out of direct light. When the leaves are well-developed and flower buds are forming, set the dish in a sunny window. Start your bulbs in October for Christmas blossoms, or in January for Easter. You can try other spring flowers such as daffodils, crocus, or tulips.

184 WHAT'S YOUR NAME?

Personalize your flower garden by planting seeds that will flower in the shape of your name.

What You'll Need: Flower box, soil, pencil, flower seeds (such as Alyssum)

Prepare the soil in a large, rectangular flower box or in a garden. Use a sharp stick or pencil to write your name in the dirt. Then sprinkle flower seeds in the marks you made. Sprinkle loose soil over the seeds and keep them watered. Soon, you'll see your name sprouting from the ground in bright green! Keep watering your name, and watch it bloom.

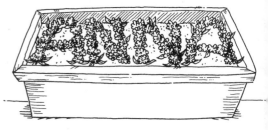

FLOWER STORY 185

Flowers are a wonderful source of material for story writing. They're fun, they're colorful, and the possibilities are endless.

What You'll Need: Field guide to plants, notebook, pen, crayons (optional)

Go exploring and observe all the different types of flowers you see in your neighborhood. The field guide can help you identify the different plants you find in nature. Remember to only go exploring during daylight and stay in a familiar area. Bring a notebook along, a pencil, and maybe some crayons so you can get the colors right. After you've done this "research" you're ready to start writing. Write a story, creating a world where only flowers exist. Make up flower people, flower buildings, anything you want. You can even draw pictures to go along with the story. Just have fun and be creative!

TREES: NATURE'S GIANTS

Trees, like all other plants, need sunlight and carbon dioxide to make their own food. In the process, trees take carbon dioxide from the air and put back oxygen. As you learn about trees with the activities in this chapter, remember how important trees are. Only use wood that has fallen from the tree. Use bark that has peeled from the tree itself, or from fallen twigs. Gather only what leaves you need and leave the rest.

COLORS IN A LEAF

186

Even green leaves have more colors than you may think!

What You'll Need: Coffee filter, scissors, leaves, coin, rubbing alcohol, jar, pencil, tape, foil

Leaves have a green pigment called chlorophyll that they use to capture sunlight. But did you know that leaves also have pigments of other colors to capture colors of light that chlorophyll misses? You can use chromatography to see the many colors in a leaf.

Cut a strip one inch wide from a coffee filter. Cut one end of the strip to a point. Place a leaf on the paper ¼ inch above the cut. Roll the edge of a coin over the leaf, pressing green leaf juice into the paper. Let the paper dry, and repeat the process with three different leaves.

Pour a ½-inch layer of rubbing alcohol into the bottom of a jar. Tape your paper strip to the middle of a pencil and hang it so that the very tip of the strip touches the alcohol. The colored strip of leaf "juices" should not touch the alcohol. You may have to adjust the length of the strip. Lay a piece of foil over the top of the jar to keep the alcohol from evaporating. Watch carefully as the alcohol moves up the filter paper, carrying the pigments along with it. In 10 to 20 minutes the colors should be separated. Do not allow them to run to the top of the paper. How many colors do you see? Could you see them in the leaf itself? The finished paper is called a chromatograph. Let it dry and use your chromatograph for a special bookmark.

HOW TO PLANT A TREE

187

Planting trees is good for the earth—but they will only live if you plant them correctly.

What You'll Need: Tree seedling, shovel, wooden stakes, elastic ties or nylon hose.

A tree seedling needs four things to live: clean air, the right amount of water, good soil, and the right amount of sunlight. When you buy the tree be sure to ask where to plant it. Some seedlings like shade, while others need more sun.

With help from an adult, dig a hole deep enough to cover the roots of the tree seedling. Use your shovel to loosen the soil in the bottom of the hole. Pile a mound of loose soil in the middle of the hole. Put the seedling into the hole up to the "root collar," spreading the roots out over the mound of dirt. Fill in with loose dirt and stomp down well to prevent large air pockets. Add more dirt until the ground is level. Be certain that all the roots are in the hole. Don't let any of them turn up in a J shape, whether they stick out of the dirt or not. This is called J-rooting and can cause the seedling to die. Water the seedling immediately. Water will help settle the soil down and fill in any remaining air pockets.

After the tree is in the ground, it still may be unstable—especially if it has a thin trunk. If you think it needs support, place two or three wooden stakes in the ground just outside of where the roots are. Use elastic ties or nylon hose to hold the tree in place. Don't tie them too tight or let them dig into the trunk. The tree should be able to move slightly in the wind. Remove the stakes as soon as the tree can support itself (usually within a year).

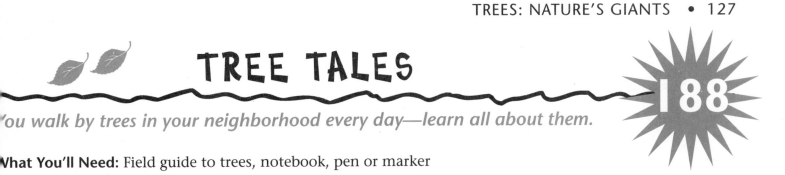

TREE TALES

188

You walk by trees in your neighborhood every day—learn all about them.

What You'll Need: Field guide to trees, notebook, pen or marker

At the library, check out a field guide to trees that grow in your area. It will have pictures, descriptions, and information about each kind of tree. Then take the field guide out into your neighborhood, and see how many of the trees you can find. Learn the name of each tree. Pay attention to what kind of leaves, seeds, and bark each tree has. Which trees have flowers, fruits, or nuts? Which trees are home to animals?

As the seasons change, keep a record of which trees' leaves change color and fall off, and which trees are the first to leaf out in the spring. You could even make your own field guide to trees in your neighborhood. Your guide could include the name of each tree, a drawing, a leaf from the tree (or tracing of a leaf), information about the tree, and details of where in the neighborhood each kind of tree can be found.

ADOPT A TREE

189

Just like people, each tree is different in its own way.

What You'll Need: Notebook, pen or marker, camera (optional)

Pick a tree that you would like to study for one year. It should be a tree that you'll be able to visit at least once a month. Get a notebook that you can use to make a diary of the tree's life for the year.

To begin, identify what kind of tree it is. Look closely at the tree's bark, leaves, any fruits or nuts, etc. Use a camera to take a picture of the tree, or draw its picture.

For the next year, visit the tree at least once a month. Each time you visit, make notes in the diary about what is happening in the life of the tree. Can you see signs of growth? Does the tree lose its leaves in winter? Does it produce flowers, berries, seed pods, or nuts? Does the tree ever show signs of stress, such as wilting leaves from lack of rain or damage from frost? Do animals make homes in your tree? Add a new picture of the tree each time you visit, too. At the end of the year, you'll have a complete report of your tree's life and growth.

HOW TALL IS IT?

190

How can you measure the height of a tree when it's really tall? Here's a neat trick to help you do it.

What You'll Need: Partner, yardstick or tape measure

You'll need a partner to do this activity. Use a yardstick to measure a straight line 60 feet away from the tree you want to measure. Then have your partner stand there and hold the yardstick straight up with the bottom touching the ground. (A yardstick will work for trees that are up to about 30 feet tall. For very tall trees, you can do this activity with a metal tape measure instead of a yardstick.)

Now walk six feet past your partner. (You'll be 66 feet away from the tree.) Lie down with your head very close to the ground at the 66-foot mark. Now look up at the tree and notice where the top of the tree comes to on the yardstick. Have your partner mark that spot. (You'll have to guide your partner to make the mark in the right place by saying, "A little lower… a little higher…" until he or she finds the right place.) The height of the tree is about 10 times the height marked on the yardstick. For example, if the mark on the yardstick is at 24 inches, the tree is about 240 inches (20 feet) tall. Calculate how tall your tree is by multiplying your yardstick measurement by 10.

TREE GROWTH

A tree will grow differently in a windy climate than in a calm climate. If a strong wind usually blows from one direction, for example, the tree's trunk and branches will grow the way the wind pushes them. If a tree grows in a thick forest, the trunk will grow more narrowly, and the branches will grow more heavily at the top of the tree, where the leaves can find light.

COUNT THE RINGS

191

Here's an easy way to figure out a tree's age.

What You'll Need: Cross section of wood showing tree rings, sandpaper

Find a tree that has been cut down. Use sandpaper to sand the surface of the stump until it is very smooth and you can see the rings. Start at the center of the stump, and count the rings. Each set of light and dark lines counts as one ring. Each ring stands for one year in the tree's life. How old was the tree? Notice that some of the rings are wider than others. Wide rings show years when the tree grew a lot. Narrow rings show years when the tree grew less. Can you think of reasons why the tree might have grown more in some years than in others?

TRUE POETREE

92

Write a poem in praise of our wooded friends.

What You'll Need: paper, pencil, markers (optional)

Trees have always been a favorite subject of poets. Here is part of a poem that Robert Frost wrote about birch trees:

When I see birches bend to left and right
Across the lines of straighter darker trees,
I like to think some boy's been swinging them.
But swinging doesn't bend them down to stay
As ice-storms do. Often you must have seen them
Loaded with ice a sunny winter morning
After a rain....
— From "Birches"

Try writing your own poem about a tree. It could be a tree you planted, or a tree you like to swing in, or even a tree in your imagination. Your poem can rhyme, or not—it's up to you! If you like, draw a picture of the tree to go with your poem.

STATE TREES

193

Every state has an official tree. Find your state tree, and learn all about it.

What You'll Need: Almanac or encyclopedia, field guide to trees, paper and pen (optional)

Look up your state in the list to find out what your state tree is. Then, look up the tree in an encyclopedia or field guide to read about it. Why do you think the tree was chosen? If you want, you can even write a story about your state tree. See if you can find your state tree in nature.

Alabama	Southern pine	**Montana**	Ponderosa pine
Alaska	Sitka spruce	**Nebraska**	Cottonwood
Arizona	Paloverde	**Nevada**	Single-leaf piñon and bristlecone pine
Arkansas	Pine	**New Hampshire**	White birch
California	California redwood	**New Jersey**	Red oak
Colorado	Colorado blue spruce	**New Mexico**	Piñon
Connecticut	White oak	**New York**	Sugar maple
Delaware	American holly	**North Carolina**	Pine
District of Columbia	Scarlet oak	**North Dakota**	American elm
Florida	Sabal palmetto palm	**Ohio**	Buckeye
Georgia	Live oak	**Oklahoma**	Redbud
Hawaii	Kukui (Candlenut)	**Oregon**	Douglas fir
Idaho	White pine	**Pennsylvania**	Hemlock
Illinois	White oak	**Rhode Island**	Red maple
Indiana	Tulip poplar	**South Carolina**	Palmetto
Iowa	Oak	**South Dakota**	Black hills spruce
Kansas	Cottonwood	**Tennessee**	Tulip poplar
Kentucky	Tulip poplar	**Texas**	Pecan
Louisiana	Cypress	**Utah**	Blue spruce
Maine	Eastern white pine	**Vermont**	Sugar maple
Maryland	White oak	**Virginia**	Dogwood
Massachusetts	American elm	**Washington**	Western hemlock
Michigan	White pine	**West Virginia**	Sugar maple
Minnesota	Red pine	**Wisconsin**	Sugar maple
Mississippi	Magnolia	**Wyoming**	Cottonwood
Missouri	Dogwood		

BARK RUBBINGS

194

Tree bark and leaves have many interesting patterns that can be "collected" by making rubbings.

What You'll Need: Large crayon or colored chalk, thin paper, trees, hair spray, craft glue, notebook, pen

Do this project on a dry day, since wet tree bark will make your paper tear. Peel the paper from a large crayon, or use a thick piece of sidewalk chalk. Press a sheet of thin paper up against the bark of a tree. Gently rub the side of the crayon or chalk on the paper until the pattern of the bark shows. Compare rubbings from different trees. Which bark patterns make the nicest rubbings? Can you tell which rubbing came from which kind of tree? For leaf rubbings, lay the leaves flat on a hard, smooth surface. Cover the leaves with paper and rub the side of the crayon or chalk on the paper.

Ask an adult to spray the pictures with hair spray to keep the chalk from smearing. Glue your rubbings in a scrapbook to make a "Bark Book." Include some interesting facts about the trees.

WHAT IS BARK?

Bark is really the skin of the tree. It surrounds the trunk and branches, and it protects the tree. Trees grow wider each year, with the newest layer of wood growing right underneath the bark. Each tree has its own unique pattern of bark, and some trees have quite unusual bark. The blistered mahogany, for example, has bark that actually blisters.

MEET A TREE

195

Here's a fun game that will test how well you know the trees in your neighborhood.

What You'll Need: Partner, blindfold

In this game you will use all your senses but sight to explore a tree, then see if you can find that tree again once your sight is restored. Play the game in a wooded area or in a park where there are lots of trees. Divide the players up into two-person teams. One person in each team puts on a blindfold. The partner turns the blindfolded person around two or three times, then leads the person in a zig-zag path to a tree. The partner must be very careful to lead the blindfolded person around dangers. The blindfolded person then has as much time as he or she wants to explore the tree, to feel the texture of the bark, find bumps or hollows, and find patches of moss or other features of the tree. When the blindfolded person is done, the partner leads him or her in a zig-zag path away from the tree, turning the blindfolded person around two or three times in the middle. The blindfolded person takes the blindfold off and tries to find the same tree. Then the partners switch places. What did you notice about your tree that you never noticed before?

LEAF SKELETONS

196

Leaf skeletons are fun to make for collections or for decoration. Here's one method you can try.

What You'll Need: Tree leaves, newspaper, old shoe brush, brown paper, craft glue

Collect fresh tree leaves. Place an entire newspaper on a table and put the leaf on top of it. Pound with an old shoe brush. Don't pound so hard that you tear the leaf, but just enough to wear away the soft green material between the leaf veins. Allow the skeleton to dry.

Mount the skeletons in a scrapbook for a collection, or use them to decorate. Cover a nature book or tree manual with brown paper and glue leaf skeletons to it

WOOD COLLECTION

197

Learn about the beauties of wood with this special collection.

What You'll Need: Saw, brush, varnish, branches or scraps of wood from lumber store, sturdy vise, sandpaper

Begin by collecting wood in a nearby forest or woodlands. Use only fallen branches, choosing solid branches about two to three inches in diameter. Have an adult saw off a six-inch length of branch. Check the leaves remaining on the branch to find out what kind of tree the branch came from. Allow the wood to dry for about two weeks. You can ask at the lumber store for small scraps of wood from trees that may not grow in your area. Try to get scraps about 2 inches square and 6 inches long.

Put your branch or wood scrap upright in a sturdy vise and have an adult help you make a two inch deep lengthwise cut down the middle. Make a second cut crosswise until your saw meets the base of the first cut. Remove the piece of wood. Sand the cut surface until smooth, then ask an adult to help you varnish it. This will beautifully highlight both the lengthwise grain and the cross-grain.

PRESERVING LEAVES

198

Make beautiful bronzed leafy branches to decorate your home.

What You'll Need: Branch cut from a leafy shrub (from spring or fall prunings), jar or bucket, glycerine (available at drug, farm, and garden stores)

With help from an adult, mix a solution of one part glycerine and two parts hot water. The amount you mix up depends on how many branches you want to preserve, but you should make enough to cover the bottom of your jar or bucket several inches deep.

Ask an adult for permission to cut branches about 18 inches long, or use prunings from shrubs in your yard. Trees or shrubs with firm, waxy leaves work the best. Carefully crush the cut ends of the branches with a hammer, peel away the bark, and stand them up in the glycerine mixture. Let them sit about three weeks. The branches will absorb the glycerine slowly through the miniature pipelines in their stems. The leaves will turn a bronze color and feel slightly greasy when preservation is complete. Wipe off the ends of the branches, and arrange in a pretty vase.

199 LEAF BATIK

The shapes of leaves inspire batik designs in this project. Make some wall hangings for your room!

What You'll Need: Leaves, green crayons, cans, pan, water, old paint brushes, fabric, cold water dye (in two colors that can mix), paraffin wax, newspaper, iron

Gather several leaves with interesting shapes. Use a green crayon to trace the shape of the leaves onto a piece of fabric. With help from an adult, put some peeled, broken green crayons in a can. Then put the can in a pan of boiling water to melt the crayons. Never melt wax or crayons directly on a stove burner. They can catch fire.

Using an old paintbrush, spread melted crayon into the leaf shape on your fabric; coat it completely. Then give it time to dry.

Mix a light-colored cold water dye with water according to the instructions on the package. Crumple your fabric and dip it in the dye. Allow to dry.

Melt paraffin wax in a can in boiling water. Paint branch shapes or any other shapes you like with the paraffin. Crumple your fabric and dip it into a darker dye. Allow to dry.

Roll your fabric hard in your hands to break up the wax and peel off as much as you can. Place the fabric between several sheets of newspaper and have an adult help you iron it. The iron will melt the wax, which will be absorbed by the newspaper. Replace the newspaper often, until most of the wax is gone.

LEAFY BLEACH PRINTS

200

Use "reverse" bleach prints to make beautiful greeting cards.

What You'll Need: Newspaper, smock or apron to cover clothes, rubber gloves, colored paper, bleach, small glass dish, paintbrush or cotton swab, assortment of leaves, markers (optional)

Caution: Bleach can irritate skin and eyes. Wear rubber gloves when doing this project, and have an adult help you. Cover your work surface with newspaper. Put a smock or apron on to protect your clothes from the bleach. Lay a sheet of colored paper out on the newspapers. Have an adult help you pour a little bleach into a small glass dish. Use an old paintbrush or cotton swab to paint the back of a leaf with bleach, then press the leaf bleach side down on the paper. Lift off the leaf. In a moment or two you will see a bleached-out print of the leaf. After you have made a nice arrangement of prints on the paper, you can hang it up for a picture, or fold it in half and make a greeting card.

HAMMERED LEAF PRINTS

201

Make a truly one-of-a-kind t-shirt, bandanna, or wall hanging!

What You'll Need: Small board (½ to one inch thick), newspaper, 100% cotton garment or fabric, leaves, waxed paper, masking tape, hammer, alum, water, salt

Cover a small board with two or three layers of newspaper. Lay your fabric on the board. If you are printing a t-shirt, open up the bottom and slip the board and newspaper inside. Arrange a variety of leaves on the fabric. Cover with a sheet of waxed paper, and tape the corners of the waxed paper to the fabric. With help from an adult, pound with the hammer until you have pounded every part of the leaf. When you are done, lift off the waxed paper. You'll see a leaf print.

To set the print: Soak for two minutes in a mixture of three tablespoons of alum in a gallon of warm water. Wring, then soak in a mixture of ¼ cup of salt in a gallon of warm water. Remove the fabric, rub off any clinging bits of leaf, wring, and let it dry. Wash by hand in cold water.

202 DOWN-TO-EARTH STARS

Twig stars make terrific natural holiday tree ornaments. Here are two different kinds of twig stars you can make to decorate your tree, a window, or any place!

What You'll Need: Small twigs (several inches long), upholstery tacks, hammer, yarn, metallic gold or silver paint (optional)

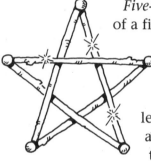

Five-pointed twig star: You'll need five twigs, all the same length. Lay them in the shape of a five-pointed star. Use gold or silver upholstery tacks to attach the twigs at each point. The tacks not only hold the star together, they add a pretty, shining touch. For a really shiny star, spray paint the twigs with metallic gold or silver paint before you tack them together.

Six-pointed twig star: You'll need three twigs, all the same length. Cross the three twigs in the middle so they make a shape like a six-pointed star. Wrap the twigs with yarn to hold them together, beginning at the center where all three twigs meet. Wrap the yarn around one stick, then the next, then the next. Keep wrapping the yarn (it will make a sort of bull's-eye pattern) until it is close to the ends of the sticks. When you're finished, tie the yarn in the back.

You can use different colors of yarn on the same star to make a colorful design. Or, turn your star into a snowflake by painting the twigs white, wrapping them with white yarn, and adding white or silver glitter.

SEQUOIAS

Some of the world's oldest and largest living trees belong to a family of trees called sequoias (named after Cherokee Indian chief "Sequoyah"). This family includes redwoods and giant sequoias. In fact, the biggest tree in the world—nicknamed "General Sherman"—is a 274-foot giant sequoia. Located in the Sequoia National Park in California, General Sherman is estimated to be between 3,000 and 4,000 years old.

LEAF STENCILS

203

Leaves make lovely artwork—and unique greeting cards and stationery.

What You'll Need: Leaves, paper, newspaper, spray paint or crayons

When using spray paint always work with an adult outside or in a well-ventilated area. Try to collect a variety of leaves with interesting shapes. Put one or more leaves on a piece of paper. Put your piece of paper on plenty of newspaper. The newspaper should be a lot bigger than your paper, so it will catch the "overspray" when you paint.

With help from an adult, use spray paint to paint the leaves. (Be sure to spray around the leaves, too.) Let the paint dry, then take away the leaves. The image is called a stencil. You can also rub crayons along the edge of your leaves instead of using spray paint to create your stencil.

You can make your leaf stencils into greeting cards. If you make stencils with light-colored paints such as yellow or silver, you can use them as stationery. You can also overlap several leaf stencils for a more intricate design.

IT'S A ROTTEN WORLD

204

There's a whole world waiting for you to explore—inside a dead log.

What You'll Need: Magnifying glass, flashlight

Take a walk in the woods and find an old, rotten log. Use a magnifying glass to explore everything that's happening in this rotten—but lovely!—little world. You may see mountains of moss, mushroom forests, and many weird little creatures. You might see ants marching along with food. Or you might see insect eggs or larvae. Can you hear any insect sounds? If you see loose bark, shine a flashlight into the crack between the bark and the log. Is anybody looking back? If the log is hollow, stand back a few feet and shine the light inside, too. Be careful, though. A hollow log might be home to a sleepy raccoon, opossum, or other animal.

It's okay to turn the log over—as long as you turn it back when you're finished. And don't take anything. You can come back again at another time of the year, and see if anything has changed.

PINE CONE FLOWERS

205

With a little creativity, you can turn ordinary pine cones into pretty flower decorations.

What You'll Need: Pine cones, knife, craft glue, cardboard, twigs or dry grass, dried leaves, large seeds or small alder cones, spray paint or glitter (optional)

Collect small pine cones outdoors. Brush off dirt or leaves. If the cones are closed, dry them in a warm oven for several hours until they open.

Have an adult cut the pine cones in half. Use a large blob of strong glue to glue the bottom halves of the pine cones to the piece of cardboard. Glue on twigs or dry grass to represent flower stems. Glue dried leaves on the twigs. Allow to dry completely before moving.

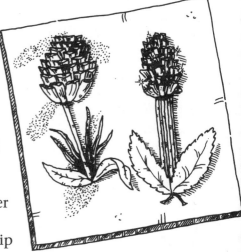

You can make smaller flowers by pulling the bracts from the cones and gluing them individually to the board in a flower shape. Use a large seed or a tiny alder cone for a center.

Pine cone flowers look nice plain, but they can be dressed up with silver or gold paint or spray paint for holiday decorations. (Have an adult help you with spray paint and work in a well-ventilated area.) You could also dip the cones in glue, then roll in glitter before gluing to the board.

CONIFERS

Pines belong to a family of trees known as conifers, which usually have leaves shaped like green needles. Conifers don't bear fruit, but they do have woody cones, such as pine cones. The cones contain the tree's seeds. You will find conifers and their cones in many parts of the world, because they can grow in cold weather, even in poor soil. Scientists think that conifers are among the world's oldest trees. Fossils of conifers have been found that are about 300 million years old.

FIRE STARTERS

206

Surprise someone with a fireplace with a basket of useful fire starters.

What You'll Need: Small pine cones, paraffin wax, metal juice can, pan, water, newspapers, waxed paper, scissors, tongs, salt, basket or bucket, ribbon

Gather small pine cones outdoors. Clean off any dirt or leaves. If the cones are closed, put them in a warm oven for several hours until they dry out and open up.

Break a block of paraffin wax into pieces and put them in a large metal juice can. Put the can in a pan of water and have an adult help you heat it slowly until the wax is melted. Never put a container of wax directly on a stove burner. It can overheat and catch fire.

Spread newspapers on the surface you are going to work on. Cut some squares of waxed paper and lay them on the newspapers. Set the pan with the wax on the newspapers (the hot water will help to keep it melted). Pick up a pine cone in the tongs and dip it in the wax. Set the cone upright on the waxed paper. Sprinkle the cone with salt. Allow the cones to cool completely. Continue with the rest of your cones. Pile them into a basket or bucket. Tie a ribbon into a big bow on the handle. One or two of these cones is enough to start a fire in the fireplace. The salt makes them burn with a bright yellow flame.

FILL 'ER UP

207

Who doesn't love the fresh scent of pine? Pine needles make a good—and good-smelling—filling for a pin cushion.

What You'll Need: Pine needles, small cloth bag, needle, thread

Start with a small cloth bag that is sewn shut on three sides. Stuff the bag very full with crushed pine needles. With adult help, use a needle and thread to sew the bag closed. This makes a lovely gift for people who sew. Or you can use it yourself to keep track of any pins or needles you need for other projects.

208 PINE CONE CREATURES

What kind of wild, imaginary animals can you make out of pine cones?

What You'll Need: Pine cone, decorations, craft glue

For each creature, you'll need one large pine cone. You'll also need an assortment of decorations (old buttons, scrap cloth, pipe cleaners, real or plastic flowers). Use these decorations to turn the pine cone into an imaginary animal. Pipe cleaners work well for creating legs. When you're done, give your creature a name, and make up a story about it.

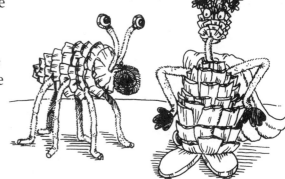

TREASURE TREE 209

Here's one way to remember your next nature trip. Make a special "tree" to display the treasures you find along the way.

What You'll Need: Nature objects, interesting branch with many side branches, coffee or peanut can, plaster of Paris, construction paper, markers, craft glue, yarn

When you are on a walk in the woods you may come across lots of interesting treasures you want to take home: cones, pretty leaves, discarded egg shells from wild bird nests, old snail shells. Rather than take everything home that attracts your eye, pick out a few of the most interesting items and make a treasure tree to display them.

Find a dead tree branch with many side limbs. Clean it off and let it dry. Mix enough plaster of Paris to nearly fill a coffee can, peanut can, or can of similar size. Stick the base of the branch into the plaster. Allow it to dry. Using markers, draw a nature setting or a decorative design on construction paper; then glue it to the can.

Use yarn to hang your treasures from the branches. You can change the decorations each time you take a walk. Remember to take only a few of the most interesting things and leave the rest for others to enjoy.

SWEET SAP

210

Maple syrup is a delicious treat straight from nature.

What You'll Need: Maple tree, drill with ½-inch bit, small tube or pipe, bucket, hammer and nail, pot, aluminum foil, butter, candy thermometer

On an early spring day, go out searching for maple trees. If the tree you find is on private property, ask for permission to tap one. Have an adult drill a hole two inches deep into the south-facing side of the tree. Drill the hole so that it slants upward into the tree slightly.

Push a piece of tubing or pipe into the hole. Hammer a nail into the tree just above the hole. Hang a bucket on the nail to catch the sap that will drip from the tubing. Cover the bucket with aluminum foil. (This should keep out any dust and dirt.) Keep in mind, it may take a few hours or longer to gather a gallon of sap.

When you have about a gallon of sap, remove the tubing and nail from the tree. Take the sap home and put it in a very large pot. With help from an adult, bring it to a boil. Much of the sap must be evaporated to make the syrup. Add a pat of butter to keep the sap from boiling over. Use a candy thermometer to check the sap's temperature. When it reaches 219°F, it's done. Strain the syrup, let it cool, and serve!

AN EARLY SPRING

211

"Forcing" is the technique used to make winter twigs bloom indoors.

What You'll Need: Winter twigs in bud, cut from flowering shrubs or trees; clippers; bucket; water; wide-mouthed vase

Check shrubs in your yard for flower buds that are just beginning to swell. Forsythia, flowering plum, flowering cherry, or pussy willows work well for this. Be sure to get permission before cutting! With adult help, cut branches about two feet long or longer if you can. Put the branches in a bucket of water right away and bring them indoors. Find a large vase with a wide mouth and fill it with water. For longest-lasting branches, put the cut end of the branch in the vase, and, holding it under the water, cut an inch off of the end. Leave your vase in a sunny window. In a week or two the twigs will burst out into blossoms.

NUTS ABOUT INK

212

You can make your own special ink using walnut shells.

What You'll Need: Eight walnuts, nutcracker, towel, hammer, saucepan, water, strainer, jar with lid, vinegar, salt

Remove the walnuts from their shells. Wrap the shells in a towel and crush them with a hammer. Put the crushed shells in a saucepan with some water. With help from an adult, heat until the water boils, then simmer the walnut shells for 45 minutes.

Let cool for 15 minutes, then pour the mixture through a strainer into a jar. Add to the jar ½ teaspoon of vinegar and ½ teaspoon of salt. Stir until the salt dissolves. Use your ink, or put the lid on the jar to store it.

BLANCHED NUTS

213

Blanching is a different and delicious way to enjoy nuts.

What You'll Need: Almonds or hazelnuts, nutcracker, 2 mixing bowls, boiling water, cookie sheet, butter, salt, pan

While this activity works best with almonds, you can try it with other nuts such as hazelnuts. Always have an adult help with blanching nuts.

Crack the nuts and remove them from their shells. Place the shelled nuts in a large steel or glass mixing bowl. Pour enough boiling water over the nuts to cover them and let them sit until the brown skins loosen. This will take about ten minutes. Have an adult help you check the nuts. When the brown skins are loose enough, remove the nuts from the water. Let them cool slightly, then slip the skins off with your fingers and place the nuts in another bowl. If the water your nuts are soaking in cools off too much and the skins become hard to slip off, add more boiling water and wait for it to cool just enough to handle. This process of skinning nuts is called "blanching."

For every pound of nuts you have, melt a tablespoon of butter in a small pan. Pour the butter over the nuts and toss until they are coated. Spread the nuts out on a cookie sheet, sprinkle with salt, and roast in a 325°F oven until golden, about ten minutes.

GROW A TROPICAL TREE

214

Enjoy a mango, papaya, or pomegranate. Then grow the tree it comes from!

What You'll Need: Tropical fruit pits (from mango) or seeds (from papaya or pomegranate), knife, vegetable brush, potting soil, flower pots, water, plastic wrap

Tropical fruit plants are fun to grow, but it takes lots of patience. Getting them to sprout is the hardest part.

Mango: Begin with a very ripe mango. Have an adult help you cut the pit from the fruit and clean it with a vegetable brush under running water. Plant the flat pit in potting soil with one edge up. Cover it completely. Keep it watered, and wait a long time. Mangoes may take three months to sprout. About one out of four will not sprout at all. Keep the plants in a humid room and away from cold windows. Once every few months, allow the soil to go completely dry.

Papaya: Have an adult help you cut the fruit open and remove the small seeds from their fleshy coating (called an *aril*). Line the bottom of a flat dish with wet paper towels and lay the seeds on it. Cover with plastic wrap and set in a warm place. When the seeds just begin to sprout, rinse them in fresh water and plant in moist potting soil. Keep the seedlings out of direct sunlight until they are about six inches tall.

Pomegranate: Prepare and sprout the seeds as you did for papayas. Pomegranates are desert plants, so keep them in a dry room.

TREES TREES TREES

215

Trees have a variety of uses in our environment. Read books—created from trees and written about them—and find out all sorts of information.

What You'll Need: One or more books about trees, pen, paper

Trees can be used for fun, as well as shelter. Where do you think tree houses come from? Did you know the oldest living tree—a 4,700 year old pine tree in California—is named "Methuselah"? Or that in Arizona there's a forest of "petrified" trees that are actually 200 million year old fossils? Find a book about trees that interests you. You might learn about acorns, leaves, or the paper-making process. Afterwards, write a story about what you discovered.

SMALL CREATURES

Insects, spiders, and all kinds of things that crawl—some people get the creeps from them, others love small critters of all kinds. In this chapter you'll find activities to help you learn about insects, spiders, worms, and other small animals. Most insects that you find are harmless. Even bees will only sting if they feel threatened. Take sensible precautions, however. Wear shoes in areas where bees are found, especially in lawns with lots of clover.

216 GOTCHA!

Have you seen movies in which someone digs a pit as a trap for a lion or tiger? You can make the same kind of trap—only yours will be for much smaller game.

What You'll Need: Glass jar, hand trowel or shovel, four flat rocks, small board

Make your safe insect trap in a place where there's likely to be a lot of bug traffic. Under a bush is good. First get a glass jar. Dig a hole that is the same size as the jar, so you can set the jar down in the hole. The lip of the jar should be about even with the ground.

Now put four small, flat rocks around the lip of the jar, and set a board on the rocks. The board will keep rain and bug-eating animals out of the jar. The rocks allow enough room for bugs to fall into the trap. Leave your trap overnight. In the morning, see what you've caught. Can you identify them? After you've studied your bug collection, be sure to let them go and fill up the hole you dug.

INSECT "COLLECTION"

217

Hunt for insects and other small creatures when the weather is warm. You can collect them harmlessly by letting them crawl onto your pencil.

What You'll Need: Small jar, magnifying glass (or a "bug box" with a magnifying lens), notebook, pencil

You can find insects and other small creatures in shrubs, trees, in the layer of leaves on the ground, and around lights at night. Capture a few insects in a jar, then gently transfer them to smaller jars or bug boxes.

Use a lens to take a closer look at your bugs. Count the number of legs first. Insects have six legs. Spiders (and a spiderlike animal called a "Harvestman") have eight legs. Isopods (often called "pill bugs") have even more. Look at the shape of the body. Does it have a "waist" (the narrow area between the thorax and abdomen) as ants and hornets do? Does it have a wide shell as beetles and many true bugs often have? What about wings? Not all insects have wings. If yours does, look at the pattern of veins, which are often used to tell one species from another.

Carefully draw each of the features in your notebook as you observe. You may want to make separate drawings of the top and bottom views, and close-up studies of wings, legs, eyes, or mouth parts. Let your bugs go as soon as you can. Then find more to add to your collection.

INVENT AN INSECT

218

What does a doodlebug look like? It's all in your imagination when you create your own crazy bug critters!

What You'll Need: Cardboard or foam egg carton, scissors, craft glue, decorations

Cut three linked sections out of the egg carton to make an insect body. Now, add the insect's other parts: head, antennae, legs (six, of course), and so on, using uncooked pasta, straws, packing peanuts, buttons—anything you find around the house. What is your bug's name? Does it have a story?

BEETLE MANIA!

219

When is a worm not a worm? When it's really a beetle! Observe the growth of these amazing insects.

What You'll Need: Mealworms, glass jar with lid, bran or oatmeal, apple or potato, water

Some creatures go through big changes during their lives. One example is the mealworm, also known as the mealy worm. You can buy these at a pet store, and watch them "grow up" into adult beetles. Put your mealworms in a glass jar with some raw bran or oatmeal. Also put in some pieces of raw apple or potato for the mealworms to eat. Sprinkle a little water in the jar, and put on the lid. (Make some small holes in the lid so air can get in.) The mealworms will morph into flour beetles. There are more than 300,000 types of beetles in the world. Some of the largest—the Goliath beetles—can grow as big as your fist!

CAUTION: TUNNEL AHEAD

220

Turn beetle tunnels into works of art when you make these one-of-a-kind rubbings.

What You'll Need: Fallen log, paper, colored pencil or crayon

When you go for a walk in the woods, look for a fallen log. If the bark has fallen off or is loose, you may see tunnels made on the log by beetles. The tunnels make interesting designs. You can preserve the designs by making a rubbing of the tunnels. Put a sheet of paper over the tunnels and rub over the paper lightly with a colored pencil or the side of the crayon. Can you trace the path the beetles made?

A CREEPY CRAWLY GAME

221

Here's a fun game you can play with your friends. The object is to be the first to make your own "Beetle."

What You'll Need: Pair of dice, drawing paper, markers

This is a game for two or more players. Each player needs a sheet of drawing paper and some markers. You will roll the dice to draw a beetle. Here's what you must roll to draw each part:

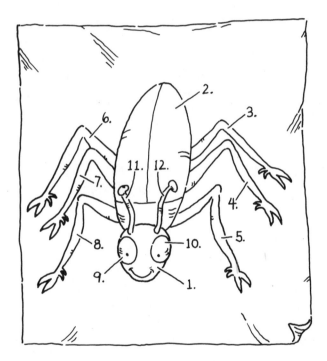

1   beetle's head
2   beetle's body
3   leg
4   leg
5   leg
6   leg
7   leg
8   leg
9   eye
10 eye
11 antenna
12 antenna

Roll both dice each time, but only draw one beetle part for each roll. Here are two examples to show you how it works:

1. Let's say you roll a 1 and a 2. You can draw either the beetle's head (1) or body (2), but not both. Or, you can draw a leg, because 1 plus 2 equals 3, and a 3 lets you draw a leg.

2. Let's say you roll a 5 and a 6. You can either draw one leg (because both 5 and 6 are for a leg), or you can add 5 plus 6 to make 11, and draw an antenna. If your beetle already has all six legs and two antennae, skip a turn.

Use different colors to make your beetle special. Whoever finishes his or her beetle first wins.

222

SPIDER "SNIFFING"

With this simple trick, you can track down spiders at night with a flashlight. Really!

What You'll Need: Flashlight, paper, pen

Your friends may think you're crazy when you say you're going spider sniffing, but give them each a flashlight and invite them to come with you and they'll be amazed.

Hunt for spiders in open fields where there are lots of shrubs. Go out at night and walk slowly through the area. Turn on the flashlight and hold it directly in front of your nose so that you can look down it. Look in the shrubs and in tall tufts of grass. You'll be able to spot spiders by the bright, jewel-like glitter of their eyes. The colors are breathtaking.

Once you've spotted a spider, get as close to it as you can. Try to figure out what kind it is. If it sits still long enough, make a drawing. Then return to the area in the daytime and notice what spiders you see. Find out if the same spiders come out in the day and the night.

BEAUTIFUL—AND DEADLY—WEBS

Garden spiders can weave invisible decorations into their spiderwebs. Invisible, that is, to people. But other insects can see the decorations, which look like daisies and marigolds. These designs make the insects come closer to the web, where they become food for the garden spiders. The best time to see a spider weave a web is in the early morning and in the early evening.

PRESERVE A SPIDERWEB

223

The spider is truly one of nature's great artists. See how you can preserve one of their masterpieces.

What You'll Need: Empty spiderweb, talcum powder, black construction paper, hair spray

To do this project, you'll need to find a spiderweb that isn't occupied. To find out if there's a spider in the web, tap it *very lightly*. If a spider is in the web, it will move and you'll see it. If the web is someone's home, find another web to preserve.

When you find an empty web, sprinkle talcum powder all over it to make it easier to see. Then, ask an adult to help you spray hair spray on a piece of black construction paper. While the spray is still wet, bring the paper up against into the web so that the web sticks to the paper. You've just preserved one of nature's great works of art.

MOTH FEEDER

224

Attract some beautiful nighttime moths with this easy feeder.

What You'll Need: Fruit juice, sugar, cotton ball, string

Did you know that there are more types of moths in the world than butterflies? Some moths even have brilliantly colored hind wings to scare off enemies. Here's how to attract them: Mix a half-cup of fruit juice with a tablespoon of sugar. Dip cotton balls in the mixture. Tie a string to each cotton ball and hang up near a window or near an outdoor light. Watch to see what kind of moths you attract. If you are lucky, you might see large Luna moths feeding at your cotton-ball "feeder."

Don't be afraid that moths coming into the house will ruin your wool clothes. Adult moths feed on nectar. Only the larvae (caterpillars) of one species of moth feed on wool, feathers, and fur. The larvae of a common beetle, the Dermestid beetle, feed on the same things. Much of the damage we blame on moths was actually caused by Dermestid beetles.

BUTTERFLY HOUSE

225

Give migrating and hibernating butterflies a helping hand by building them a place to live.

What You'll Need: Hand saw, pine lumber (6"×½"×7'), scrap of pine (8" wide), hammer, nails, pieces of tree bark or floral moss

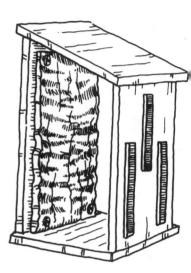

When butterflies migrate they need to find shelter from bad weather. Usually they seek shelter in cracks of trees or buildings. Some butterflies will hibernate in the winter and need shelter to protect them from winter cold. You can build a butterfly house to help migrating and hibernating butterflies. Be sure to have an adult help with this project.

First, cut pine boards to the following dimensions:

Two sides: 6"×18" Cut the top at an angle so that one side is 18 inches long and the other side is 17 inches long.

One back: 4½"×18"

One front: 4½"×17"

One bottom: 4½"×6"

One top: 7"×7"

Next, cut three 12-inch long slits in the front. Make the slits one inch wide, with one several inches higher than the other two. (See illustration.) Nail the bark or moss to the back piece to give the butterflies something to cling to.

Lay the back down, bark side up, and stand one of the side pieces up against it with the longer sides in back. Hold and nail in place. Do the same with the other side. Put the front in between the two side pieces and nail in place. Nail on the bottom and the top. Mount the house on a post in the shade.

BUTTERFLY FUN

226

Why should you crawl when you can fly? Watch a caterpillar turn into a butterfly.

What You'll Need: Aquarium or glass jar with lid, potting soil, stick, caterpillar, leaves

Butterflies come in all kinds of beautiful varieties. Here's how you can raise your very own. Make a caterpillar hatchery in a large glass jar or aquarium. Put a layer of potting soil in the bottom of the container. Put a stick in the soil, and lean the top of the stick against the side of the container. You're now ready to find a caterpillar. You'll find them feeding on leaves of plants like cabbages. When you find one, pay attention to what kind of leaves it is eating. (Different caterpillars eat different plants.) Gently pick up the caterpillar and plenty of the leaves, and put them in the hatchery. Put a lid or cover on the hatchery, but make sure air can get in.

Be sure to check on your caterpillar every day. Caterpillars have huge appetites! In its new home, the caterpillar will keep munching leaves (make sure it always has some) until it begins making a cocoon (also called a chrysalis). The caterpillar will come out of its cocoon as a butterfly. You won't recognize it! When that happens, take the hatchery outside and let the new creature fly away.

FLYING FLOWERS

If you have ever read Robert Frost's poetry in school, you may know what he meant by the term "flying flowers." Frost was referring to butterflies, which many people consider the most beautiful insects. There are spring butterflies, and there are summer butterflies, each having favorite plants and flowers that they like to eat.

HONEYBEE COOKIES

227

Take a break from your insect exploring to bake these cookies—the perfect treat for a buzzzy day!

What You'll Need: Electric mixer, 2 medium bowls, ¾ cup shortening, ½ cup sugar, ¼ cup honey, 1 egg, ½ teaspoon vanilla, 2 cups all-purpose flour, ½ cup cornmeal, 1 teaspoon baking powder, ½ teaspoon salt, plastic wrap, cookie sheets, decorations: yellow and black icing, gummy fruit

In an electric mixer beat shortening, sugar, and honey at medium speed until fluffy. Add egg and vanilla; mix until well blended.

Combine flour, cornmeal, baking powder, and salt in medium bowl. Add to shortening mixture, mix at low speed until well blended.

Cover with plastic wrap; refrigerate several hours or overnight.

Preheat oven to 375°F. Divide dough into 24 equal sections. Shape each section into oval-shaped ball. Place 2 inches apart on ungreased cookie sheets.

Bake 10 to 12 minutes or until lightly browned. Cool 2 minutes on cookie sheets. Remove to wire racks; cool completely.

Decorate with icings and gummy fruit to create honeybees. Makes 2 dozen cookies.

How Many Feet Was That?

Many people confuse centipedes and millipedes. That's because both of them have lots of legs! Centipedes (whose name means "100 feet") have only one pair of legs for each of their body segments. Millipedes, however, can have many more legs than centipedes.("Millipede" means "1,000 feet"—but they don't really have that many.) A centipede also has a pair of pincers (or claws) in front that can inject poison into its enemies or prey. A millipede defends itself with a foul-smelling liquid—just like a skunk!

THE MOSQUITO

One of the least popular insects in the world has to be the mosquito. Their bites can be itchy and painful. When the mosquito "bites," however, it is actually stabbing through a person's skin with a sharp body part called a "stylet." The mosquito then pulls out some of the person's blood, and leaves behind saliva. Since many people are allergic to the mosquito's saliva, the spot of the "bite" itches.

WHAT'S THE BUZZ?

228

What do bees and ballerinas have in common? Learn about the amazing antics of the busy little bee.

What You'll Need: Field guide to insects or other reference book

You probably already know that each kind of animal has its own language. Birds have all different kinds of calls and songs. Dogs bark, cats meow, and dolphins "click." And what about bees? Well, they use their own kind of sign language. They communicate with one another by dancing. For example, a honeybee that has found food tells other bees about it by flying in a circle if the food is nearby, and in a figure eight if it's far away.

At the library, check out a field guide to insects or a book about bees. Learn more about how bees communicate. Spend some time watching bees. Finally, see if you can dance like a bee. Try imitating the different patterns you've read about.

OBSERVING WORMS

229

Worms are a necessary part of nature's delicate balance.

What You'll Need: Flashlight, worms, paper, strong magnifying glass, notebook, pen

For this activity, you'll need to find some good-sized worms to observe. You can dig in soft, moist garden soil to find lots of small ones. To find big nightcrawlers, go out onto a healthy lawn at night with a flashlight. You might try lifting a large stone or flowerpot, or digging under the ground's surface.

Once you've got your worm, wet your fingers and run them down both sides of the worm at once. You may be surprised to feel short, stiff bristles (called "setae") that help the worm move through the soil. Put the worm on a dry piece of paper and let it crawl. You will hear a faint scratching noise as the setae rub on the paper. Notice how the worm moves. Strong muscles running up and down the body shorten it, while ring-shaped muscles squeeze it to make it longer. Write down your findings and make drawings of your worm. Always put the worms back where you found them when you are done.

WIGGLY WORKERS

230

Earthworms have been called "a gardener's best friend." Find out why.

What You'll Need: Wide-mouth glass jar, garden soil, peat, sand, water, earthworms, dead leaves, paper bag

To make a wormery, first get a large jar that has a wide opening. Put in a layer of soil, a layer of peat, and a layer of sand. Water the soil well. Now dig some worms from a garden and put them in your wormery. Don't bury the worms! They'll take care of that themselves. But do cover the worms with some dead leaves. Set a paper bag over the top of the jar. This will keep out light, but let in the oxygen that worms need. Now put the jar in a cool place out of direct sunlight.

Keep your wormery damp and keep an eye on the earthworms. Can you guess why gardeners like earthworms? It's because they digest and pass soil through their bodies, loosening the soil and mixing nutrients. Plants grow better in looser soil with plenty of oxygen. Once you've seen the worms work, put them back where you got them.

HOLD ON TIGHT!

If you were searching for a big nightcrawler to use as bait for fishing, you might have a hard time pulling it out of the ground. This creature's body has 150 rings or segments, with eight little bristles on each segment. So, it has 1,200 little feet to grab onto the dirt, and to hold on tightly!

231

DECOMPOSERS

Is it the end or just the beginning? Find out when you watch decomposers do their work.

What You'll Need: Apple

In nature, everything happens in cycles. For example, water moves in a cycle from rivers to oceans to clouds, back to Earth in the form of rain, which runs back into rivers, and so on. In this activity, you'll see part of the life cycle of plants. Decomposition is the last stage of the life cycle of a plant. But, in a way, it's also the first stage. That's how cycles work.

Take a few bites out of an apple. Put the apple outdoors in a damp area away from houses and people. It will also need to be a place where animals won't bother the apple. Leave the apple outside overnight.

The next day, go see the apple. Has it started to decompose? Do you see any decomposers at work? Decomposers are living things that break down the apple and turn it back into soil. Decomposers like flies and worms may be gross, but they're important!

The apple is made of elements such as carbon, hydrogen, oxygen, etc. It's no coincidence that soil is made of the same elements. Decomposers turn the apple back into soil, so new apples can grow. In fact, if no one disturbs your apple, and if the weather is right, the seeds in that apple just might sprout into new apple trees, putting down roots in soil that was once your apple. It's just one of nature's many cycles.

THE UNDERSIDE OF NATURE

232

There's a whole side of nature that no one ever sees—the underside! See what lives under a rock.

Take a walk in a wooded area. When you come across a big rock, turn it over. You'll be amazed at the busy world that's under there. Check out all the creatures that live under the rock.

Do you recognize any of them? You might find beetles, worms, or centipedes. You might even find an entire ant colony hidden from sight! Many types of creatures will make their home under a rock during the day and come out at night, when they are protected by darkness. After your visit, be sure to put the rock back exactly as it was, so life on the underside can get back to normal.

JUMPIN' JIMINY!

233

Most insects don't like cold weather, but snow fleas love it!

What You'll Need: Snow fleas, paper, pen, reference books

Have you ever been out on a winter day and seen what looked like pepper sprinkled on the snow? Have you seen that pepper start to jump up and down? If so, you've seen snow fleas.

The good news is, snow fleas aren't really fleas. But it's easy to see how they got their name, since they look like tiny fleas when they bounce around in the snow. Snow fleas are also called springtails, and that's an even better name for them. You see, they have a tail-like feature that works like a pogo stick. You might say that springtails have a built-in ejection seat!

If you've never seen snow fleas, look for them under trees on sunny winter days. Just look for what looks like specks of pepper that are jumping up and down!

Why do you suppose snow fleas act that way? Make a list of other creatures that jump up and down? Although these creatures share the same behavior, they may jump up and down for different reasons.

Look up the creatures on your list in a reference book. Then make a chart of the information you find. Remember to include the type of creature, the origin, and the size, as well as the reasons behind the jumping behavior. You may even want to draw pictures to go along with your chart.

LET'S GO SKATING

234

If you're lucky, you've had the chance to go skating on a frozen pond in the winter. But you've never gone skating on a pond in summer—unless you're a water strider.

Water striders are insects that live on the surface of a pond or river. They have long, skinny legs that allow them to spread their weight (which isn't much!) over the water's surface, so they don't sink. With an adult, go to a nearby pond or stream, and see if you can spot any water striders. Look in places where the water is calm. If you do, you'll understand why they're also called "pond skaters." Just don't try it yourself!

MAKING TRACKS

235

You may not think that snails can do much. But with a little help from you, they can be artists!

What You'll Need: Garden snails, black construction paper, talcum powder

Have a snail hunt and see if you can collect several snails. (Be gentle! Those shells may be fragile!) Snails are nocturnal, which means they like to sleep during the day and come out at night. You can usually find them sleeping in damp dark places, such as under a rock. One way to catch snails is to put a large clay flower pot upside down, with one side propped up, overnight in a garden.

Once you've found some snails, put them on a sheet of black construction paper and let them do what they do—crawl around. You'll be able to see the slimy trail they leave. When the paper is criss-crossed with snail tracks, carefully put the snails back where you found them. Sprinkle talcum powder on their tracks. Tap off the excess talcum powder, and admire your snail art.

LIGHT UP THE NIGHT

236

Fireflies have their own, built-in flashlights. Catch and observe some of these amazing creatures.

What You'll Need: Fireflies, glass jar

As you may know, fireflies are also called lightning bugs. Those tiny, blinking lights add beauty and mystery to a summer night. But, for fireflies, they also serve a purpose. They're flashing a code to try to find a mate. In fact, different kinds of fireflies have different colors of lights and blink them at different speeds.

It's fun to catch and watch fireflies—as long as you're gentle and you let them go after a few minutes. You're likely to find fireflies hovering over tall grass on summer evenings. Hold up a big glass jar, and move toward the flashing lights. When you capture a firefly, put your hand over the top of the jar. Time the flashes to see how far apart they are. Then catch another firefly, and see if the flashes are timed the same—or different.

FIND THE HIDING PLACE

237

If you've ever looked closely at small plants and trees, you may have noticed bumps on their leaves or stems. Those bumps—called "galls"—are made by tiny insects.

What You'll Need: Galls, glass jar

If the gall contains holes, it tells you that the bugs "holed up" there have left. A gall that doesn't have holes is still hiding some insects. Go for a walk and look for galls on plants and trees. Oak trees are a favorite hiding place of gall-making insects. If you find some galls without holes, pick the part of the plant with the gall. Put it in a glass jar and cover the jar loosely, so air can get in. Keep an eye on the gall. If you're lucky you might see tiny bugs coming out of hiding. After they do, take the jar outside and gently put its contents on the ground.

ANT FARM

238

This ant farm comes with a moat to prevent escapes!

What You'll Need: Gallon glass jar, cardboard, scissors, stapler, water, sand, spoon, pie pan, small block of wood, cheesecloth, rubber band, ants, bits of bread

Clean and dry a one-gallon glass jar. Measure the jar from the base to just below the shoulder and cut a long strip of cardboard that wide. Bend it into a cylinder the same size as the mouth of the jar. Staple the ends together and put the cylinder into the jar.

Next, add water to sand until it is just barely moist. Spoon the sand into the space between the cylinder and the jar. Set a block of wood in the middle of a pie pan and place the jar on top of it. Fill the pan with water. This forms a moat that will foil any ants that try to escape. Cover the top of the jar with several layers of cheesecloth held in place with a rubber band.

Catch ants outdoors and put them on top of the sand of your ant farm. You should only put in ants from the same colony, so try to catch all of your ants around the same location. Give them a few bread crumbs every few days to eat, and only feed them when their food has been eaten. Keep in mind that an ant colony cannot survive or reproduce without a queen (who lives underground and is hard to catch), so your ants are probably worker ants. You will need to set them free or they will eventually age and die.

CREATURE FEATURE

239

There are lots of interesting, creepy, crawly creatures! Which is your favorite?

What You'll Need: One or more books or poems on small creatures, paper, pen

If you could be any kind of small creature, what would you be? An ant? A dragonfly? A spider? Check out some books from your library about your favorite small creatures. Then write your own story or poem about a day in the life of an insect, spider, or other small creature: Where does it live? How does it work? What does it eat? Be creative and have fun!

THE ANIMAL KINGDOM

From the lion's roar to the mouse's squeak to the neighborhood dog's bark—animals sure have a way of getting our attention! This chapter has great activities and crafts about all kinds of animals. Learn about your favorite animals, whether they're pets, familiar wild animals, or exotic animals you might have never even heard of! Use your craft skills to help others learn about protecting animals all over the world.

240 IT'S AN ORANGU-PHANT!

Nature has quite an imagination, wouldn't you say? See if you do, too, by inventing an animal.

What You'll Need: Magazines, scissors, glue, construction paper, pen

There are some pretty weird-looking animals in nature. Take the platypus, for example. It has a bill and webbed feet like a duck, a furry body and flat tail like a beaver, and it lays eggs like a turtle. Then there's the echidna, an anteater that is covered with prickly spines like a porcupine. Nature has also "invented" lizards with three eyes, frogs that glide, and pigs with beards!

See if you can outdo nature. Look through some old magazines to find pictures of animals. Cut out different parts of different animals to invent a new creature. Make a collage of your creature by gluing the different parts together on a piece of construction paper. Once your creation is complete, give it a name and a "biography." Write a story telling how this creature came to be, where it lives, and what it eats. Tell how each of its parts helps the creature survive.

WHO'S OUT THERE?

241

Identify some of the creatures you share your neighborhood with.

What You'll Need: Reference book or field guide, notebook, pen

If you've ever awakened in the middle of the night and heard strange animal noises coming from "out there," you know that you are not alone. Go to the library, check out a field guide, and learn what animals live in your area. Then take a nature hike and see if you can meet some of your neighbors.

The best time to do this is either just after it gets light in the morning, or at dusk. Most animals are more active at those times than they are during the day. Watch for signs of animals, such as paw prints or animal homes. Keep a journal of your animal sightings.

Try this activity at different times of the year. Do you see different animals during different seasons? When do they gather food or build new homes? When do you see baby animals?

Remember: Never approach or touch a wild animal. Most wild animals are afraid of humans and, if threatened, will try to protect themselves—sometimes by biting. Also, wild animals carry diseases. If you see an animal that seems to be sick or injured, call your city's animal control department or the police. Don't try to help the animal yourself.

TAKE AN ANIMAL CENSUS

242

Figure out the animal population of a spot near you.

What You'll Need: Wooden stakes or sticks, string, paper, pen

A census is a count of how many people—or animals—live within an area. In an open field or wooded area, use four stakes or sticks to mark off a square that is one meter on each side. Then run string around the four sticks to make an actual square. Take a census of all the animals inside the square. Look carefully to make sure everybody gets counted. Look under rocks. (Be polite and put the rocks back when you're done counting.) Look in any bushes or trees. Make a record of your census, telling how many of each kind of insect, spider, and other animal you found living there.

ANIMAL TRACK STAMPS

243

If you know what to look for, you can read animal tracks like a story. Make a "rubber" stamp, then invent your own critter tales.

What You'll Need: Small blocks of wood (about 2"×2"×1"), adhesive moleskin (found in the foot care sectio of the drug store), ink pen, field guide to animals, scissors, stamp pad

Turn the moleskin to the paper side. With an ink pen, draw the outline of animal tracks. (Use the pictures in a field guide as patterns.) With adult supervision, cut out the shapes with sharp scissors, then peel off the paper backing. Stick the shapes onto a small block of wood. Press your stamp on the stamp pad and stamp away!

Try making a set of tracks that tell a story. You could show one animal following another, or space tracks farther apart to show an animal running A cluster of tracks in a small area could show that the animal had found something to eat or something else of interest.

BE A TRACKER

244

Beat the winter blahs! A great time to learn to read and follow animal tracks is after a snowfall.

What You'll Need: Field guide to animals that shows their tracks

Depending on where you live, you may find the tracks of dogs, cats, birds, opossums, raccoons, rabbits, squirrels, deer, coyote, or other animals. Use a field guide to help you identify tracks. If you live in a neighborhood with lots of dogs, have fun trying to figure out which dog made which tracks. Use the size of the tracks as a clue, and also pay attention to how deep the tracks are. (The deeper the track, the heavier the animal.)

See how far you can follow the tracks. Tracks may lead you to an animal's home. See if the tracks lead to source of food. Two sets of tracks may be evidence of a chase.

PLASTER CASTER

245

Make a long-lasting collection of animal tracks.

What You'll Need: Long strip of cardboard, paper clips, plaster of Paris, water, mixing container, spoon, acrylic paint (optional)

Find a muddy place where animals often visit. Stream banks and marshes are best since water attracts a wide variety of animals. You can also make a muddy patch in your backyard and bait it with a little food.

Once you find a clear track, make a collar of stiff cardboard to fit around it. Paper clip the ends of the cardboard together and push the collar into the mud around the track. Mix plaster of Paris with water until it is pourable but not too thin. Pour about an inch of plaster into the collar. Let it set before removing. Handle the cast gently until you can get it home and let it dry completely. When it is dry, you can paint the track with acrylic paints if you want.

NIGHTWATCHING

246

You may be surprised how many animals live near your house.

What You'll Need: Flashlight, red cellophane

Woods, parks, fields, and other places are often full of animals we're not aware of because they come out at night. If you are quiet and still, you can see some of these night creatures.

Go with an adult, and find a safe place in the woods where you can sit and watch. Make sure the spot is quiet and well away from any bright lights. During the daytime, you can remove sticks and rocks, so the spot will be more comfortable. You can also lay a folded blanket out.

Before going out, cover the front of a flashlight with two layers of red cellophane. Red light won't affect your night vision, but it is hard for most animals to see. Go outside and wait a few minutes for your eyes to become adjusted to the dark. Turn on your flashlight and go to your spot. Allow yourself at least a half an hour to sit. Listen carefully for any animal noises. If you hear something, you can slowly move the beam of your flashlight toward it, but try to see it without the aid of the flashlight first.

FLASH!

247

Help someone learn about the wild world of animals.

What You'll Need: 4"×6" index cards, pen, reference books, magazines, scissors, glue, markers (optional)

Make some flash cards using 4"×6" index cards. For each flash card, write a fact or two about an animal on one side of the card. (Read reference books and magazines to learn about animals.) On the other side of the card, put the animal's picture and name. You can cut pictures out of old magazines, or draw them yourself.

You can use your flash cards to help your friends learn about animals. First read them the fact, and then ask them to name the animal. (Example: I live in the water, but I'm not a fish. I'm the world's largest mammal. Who am I? Answer: a blue whale!) Or show them the pictures while covering up the animals' names, and have them guess the names. See if you can stump them, or have them make some cards and see if they can stump you.

HOME SWEET HOME

248

If you look in the right places, you can often see animals in their homes.

Take a hike and see how many animal homes you can find. Look in trees for birds' nests, squirrels' holes, and wasps' nests. Hollows inside trees are squirrels' favorite kind of home, but squirrels sometimes build nests out of leaves high in a tree. You can see these nests in the winter after the leaves fall.

Even if you live in a city or suburb, it's likely that there are opossums and/or raccoons living in your neighborhood. Opossums may "den" in a hollow log or under a bush or house. Raccoons like to live in hollow trees. But when they live near humans, raccoons often like to be *very* near humans. They often spend their days sleeping hidden in attics or garages, or under porches. You'll know you've found a den if you find fur the animal has shed and maybe some tidbits of leftover food. Tell an adult so the animal can be safely removed and taken to a more natural area. Unless an animal has invaded your house, never disturb an animal's home. It could harm the animal, and it could be unhealthy for you.

Z IS FOR ZOO

249

An ABC book about animals makes a great gift—it's like giving someone a trip to the zoo.

What You'll Need: Notebook, pen or pencil, camera (optional), old magazines, scissors, markers

An ABC book is a book that has one sentence or one page for each letter of the alphabet. A visit to the zoo makes a great topic for an ABC book. The next time you go to the zoo, take a notebook with you. Write down the name of each animal you see. Also write down one interesting fact about each animal. Draw a sketch or bring a camera and take pictures of the animals, too.

When you get back home, make your ABC book. For each letter, think of an animal that starts with that letter. Put its picture on the page. (If you didn't take photos or draw pictures, you can cut pictures out of old magazines.) Then write the animal's name and a fact about the animal. For example, if you saw an aardvark, you might write: The name "aardvark" means "earth pig."

If you come to a letter that you don't have an animal for, think of an object at the zoo that begins with that letter. For "H," you could write about the hot dog you had for lunch! Try to think of an animal or a word for every letter of the alphabet. When you're done, you'll have a book about the zoo, from A to Z!

ANIMAL DEFENSES

All animals need to protect themselves in the wild. Some are fast and can outrun predators. Others have claws or sharp teeth. Still others have developed unique forms of defense. Turtles have armorlike shells for protection. The porcupine grows sharp quills that ward off an opponent. And the skunk uses a nasty-but-effective method—it squirts smelly liquid on an enemy!

POLAR BEAR WARMTH

250

How do polar bears stay warm in the freezing cold of the Arctic? Use coffee to find the answer.

What You'll Need: Coffee, two glass jars, cloth, plastic wrap, food thermometer

Pour one cup of strong black coffee into each of two clear glass jars. Let the jars sit until the coffee is room temperature. Cover one jar with a piece of white cloth, and the other jar with a piece of clear plastic wrap. Then put both jars in the sun for an hour or more. Use a food thermometer to check the temperature of the coffee in each jar. Which is warmer? Can you explain why?

And now for the polar bear's secret: Polar bears are not really white. If they were, they couldn't stay warm in their Arctic habitat. As you just learned, white reflects sunlight and the heat that comes with it. The hairs in a polar bear's coat are clear. The hollow center of each hair soaks up light from the sun, and the light filters out the sides. That's what makes polar bears *look* white. Each clear hair carries heat from the sun down to the polar bear's skin. Its skin is black, which means it soaks up heat to keep the bear warm. A polar bear is like the plastic-covered coffee in your experiment: Clear on the outside, black on the inside—and plenty warm!

WHAT HAIRY FEET YOU HAVE!

While you probably knew that polar bears live in cold climates, did you know that their feet have hair on the bottom of them? Well, they do—that's what keeps the bears from slipping on the ice.

BE AN EAGER BEAVER

251

Beavers build their dens with mud and sticks. You can build a miniature beaver den from common items.

What You'll Need: Toothpicks or twigs, modeling clay, shoe box, rocks, leaves, saucer, plastic cup

Use your hands to mix a lot of toothpicks or twigs into the clay. (Be careful not to poke yourself!) Then shape the clay into a den (like a small cave) with an opening.

Now, get a large shoe box or other shallow box. (If you use a shoe box, you may want to cut down the sides.) You're going to make a beaver habitat and place the beaver den in it. At one end of the box, pile up some more clay, and place the beaver den on it. The den should be a couple of inches above the bottom of the box. Place more clay, small rocks, leaves, and twigs all over the bottom of the box.

Beavers build tunnels from their dens into nearby ponds. Put a small, shallow container in the bottom of

the shoe box as a pond. (A small saucer that goes under a flower pot makes a good pond.) Use a small plastic cup as your tunnel. Cut the bottom out of the cup. Put the bottom of the cup into the den opening. Use clay to attach the cup to the den and also to cover the top of the cup, so it looks like a tunnel. The top of the cup should be in the pond.

With this ingenious home, beavers can scurry down to the pond to get water and plants for dinner, then go back home without ever venturing outside where predators might see them.

GET A RACCOON'S-EYE VIEW

252

Find out what nature looks like to a raccoon.

Did you know raccoons are related to bears and are only found in North and South America? They are extremely good swimmers—and they even "wash" their food before they eat it!

Go on a hike, but do it the raccoon way: Walk on all fours (or hands and knees), and be very, very quiet. What do you see at this level that you never noticed before? What do you smell? (If you're a good raccoon, you'll be sniffing for anything that smells good to eat.) What do you hear? You probably won't see a raccoon on your hike, since they sleep in trees during the day and are most active at night.

FOX AND MOUSE GAME

253

Animals often use their sense of hearing to help them find food and avoid danger. This game will help you and your friends sharpen your ears.

The fox is one of nature's most clever animals. It uses its large ears to help hunt for food. Here's how you can be as cunning as a fox.

Have a group of friends—at least four—stand in a circle. Pick one person to be the fox. That person will stand in the middle of the circle with his or her eyes closed. Have a mouse (one of the people in the circle) walk in an inner circle around the fox and then return to his or her place in the outer circle. The fox must try to guess who the "mouse" was, using sounds as clues. If the fox guesses correctly, the mouse takes a turn as the fox.

Many animals use their hearing skills to protect themselves in the wild. Rabbits have big ears so they can listen for danger and quickly run away. Can you think of some ways that your ears help you?

WALK LIKE THE ANIMALS

254

This is a fun activity to do with a group of friends at a park or beach. Have races where everybody runs like a certain animal.

What You'll Need: Group of friends

Decide on a starting and finishing line, and try the following animal races:

Crab race: Racers are on all fours (hands and feet), and must move sideways.

Chimp race: Racers hold their ankles with their hands or drag their knuckles on the ground.

Frog race: Racers squat in frog position and hop.

Can you think of other animals to imitate in your races?

MOOSE FOR A MOMENT

255

Imagine walking around all day with a pile of wood on your head that is as much as six feet wide and weighs 85 pounds. That's about the size and weight of a moose's antlers!

What You'll Need: Four-foot long stick, two plastic milk jugs, string, construction paper (optional)

Here's how to make and wear your own antlers: Get a stick or dowel that's about four feet long. That will be the "rack" part of your antlers. Now, on each side of your "rack," you'll need some "points." You can get the idea by tying an empty plastic milk jug to each side of the stick. Or, make antler points out of construction paper.

When you've made your antlers, hold them on top of your head. Be careful where you turn around. Can you walk through your bedroom door? Remember, if you were really a moose, those antlers would weigh 85 pounds (and you would weigh about a half of a ton), and you'd spend some of your time running at top speed through thick forest. You get the idea: It's not easy being a moose!

MAD ABOUT MOOSE

The moose is one of the largest of North America's wild land animals. It is about as tall as a horse, and a male moose (known as a bull moose) can weigh up to 1,100 pounds! As big as it is, the moose is also a swift animal, able to outrun a horse.

REAL LIVE DRAGONS

Do dragons really exist? Well, yes and no. For years people living near the small Indonesian island of Komodo told stories of the giant "dragons" that populated the island. Then, in 1912, a group of explorers discovered that the dragons were really large monitor lizards. In fact, the Komodo dragon is the world's largest lizard—it can grow to be more than 11 feet long. It spends its day living in a cave, just like a real dragon!

256 TERRIFIC TURTLES

Turtles have been around since the days when dinosaurs walked the earth—millions of years ago. Here's how to make your own turtle "pet rock."

What You'll Need: Rock, small pebbles, stone, craft glue, paint

Do you know the difference between a turtle and a tortoise? A turtle refers to all shelled reptiles, but a tortoise is a type of turtle that lives entirely on the land. Turtles come in all sizes. Some can grow as big as 1,200 pounds and live as long as 100 years.

To create your turtle, begin with a medium-size rock. This will be your turtle's body and shell. Then find four similar-size pebbles to use for the feet. Glue the pebbles onto your rock using strong glue, leaving room at one end for the head. Now find a stone slightly larger than the feet to be your turtle's head, and glue it in place. Let the glue dry.

Once the glue dries, it's time to decorate your pet. Paint a face, and then decide what kind of design you want your turtle's shell to have. Many turtles have lovely, colorful designs on their shells. (You can look in a reference book to see some examples.) Or you can come up with your own design. Maybe you want a spiral or checkerboard pattern on your turtle's shell.

FROG RAFT

257

Ahoy! Who wants to go for a sail on a miniature raft just for frogs?

What You'll Need: Board (18 inches long, one-inch thick), candle or small electric lantern, 2-inch-long nail (if using candle), plastic bag (if using lantern), heavy twine, large screw eye

If you have access to a pond you can visit at night, go frog "hunting." Shine a flashlight out over the pond and watch for glittering frog eyes. Then launch a frog raft and see if you can get any passengers.

With help from an adult, insert a screw eye in one end of your board and tie the end of your twine to it. For a light, drive a nail all the way through the board. Stick a candle on the pointed end that comes through the board. If your nights are too breezy for candle flames, omit the nail and candle, and use a small battery-powered lantern instead. It won't be as attractive as a flickering candle flame, but it may still attract frogs. Seal the lantern in a heavy plastic bag, then tie it to the board. Put the raft in the water and give it a push, then wait quietly for frogs to jump aboard. See how many passengers your raft will attract.

AN ORANGE FROG?

Yes, it's true. While most frogs you see are green or brown, they come in all types of colors, including red, orange, blue, and black. It's also possible for the common green frog to look orange if that frog has too much yellow pigment in his skin.

GOING BATTY

258

Ever heard the expression "blind as a bat"? Bats do have poor vision, but they have their own special way of "seeing." Find out how by playing bat tag.

What You'll Need: Blindfold

Bats get around by using "echolocation." (Break it into two smaller words, *echo* and *location*.) Bats fly around squeaking all the time. Their squeaks "bounce" off objects and echo back to the bat's big ears. Bats use the echo to tell the location of the object. This works so well that they can zero in on (and eat) hundreds of mosquitoes in a single night.

To play bat tag, you'll need a group of people. You'll also need a big, open area with no trees or other things to run into! Choose someone to be the bat. The others will be insects. Blindfold the bat. The other players spread out. Once the game begins, the bat begins to squeak. The player that is facing the bat should squeak back, like an echo. The bat can move around, but the other players do not move. The bat has to find and tag the other players by listening to their squeaks. When each "insect" is tagged, it stops squeaking. The last "insect" to be tagged is the bat next time.

CLEAN AS A...BAT?

Bats have a terrible reputation, and lots of people think they're unclean. But bats wash themselves like cats do, licking their fur very carefully. They comb themselves with their claws, too, and they clean out their ears with a knuckle. So, actually, bats are very clean animals.

CRITTERS-IN-HOLES

259

Critters you can eat: Yummy! You'll love making and eating these sweet, tasty, gooey treats!

What You'll Need: 48 chewy caramel candies coated in chocolate; knife; 48 pieces of candy corn; vanilla icing; 1 package (20 ounces) refrigerated peanut butter cookie dough; shortening; muffin tins

Have an adult help you cut a slit into the side of one caramel candy. Carefully insert a piece of candy corn into slit. Repeat with remaining caramel candies and candy corn. To create eyes, dot icing on top of each piece of candy.

Preheat oven to 350°F. Grease 12 (1¾-inch) muffin cups.

Remove dough from wrapper according to package directions. Have an adult help you cut dough into 12 equal slices; then, cut each slice into 4 equal sections. Place one section of dough into each muffin cup.

Bake 9 minutes. Remove from oven and immediately press 1 decorated carmel candy into center of each cookie. Remove to wire racks; cool completely. Repeat until you've baked and decorated all cookies. Makes 4 dozen "critters."

WHERE'S YOUR SKIN?

We take our skin for granted. When we grow bigger, so does our skin. But snakes, on the other hand, actually outgrow their skin. When this happens, the snake needs to shed (or "slough") its skin. It grows a new, larger layer of skin underneath the old one to take its place. Snakes will shed their skin several times in a single year.

SALAMANDER TERRARIUM

260

Make a cool, comfortable home for a pet salamander.

What You'll Need: Salamander (from a pet store), aquarium, gravel, moss from woods, water, dechlorinator (optional), insects as food

Salamanders are sold in pet shops. You can find them in woods and ponds, too, but never take one from the wild. Wild animals need to be in their own homes. Before bringing a salamander home, read about them and find out how to care for them.

Rinse aquarium gravel in a sieve before using. Cover the bottom of an aquarium with one inch of gravel. Mound clean gravel up on one side to form a hill about six inches high and as wide as half the length of the aquarium. Add enough water to make a pond about three inches deep, leaving the top of the mound out of water. (If you use tap water, add a dechlorinator, or let the aquarium sit for 24 hours to allow the chlorine to evaporate.) Cover the top of the mound with forest moss and dampen it. Put a glass or plastic cover on the aquarium to maintain humidity.

The aquarium is now ready for your guests. Offer them crickets, small worms, or mealworms to eat, or catch insects outdoors to feed them. Try several foods to see what they like best.

DECK THE TREE

261

Wild animals will appreciate a tree full of treats—especially in the winter.

What You'll Need: Tree, animal treats, rake

This activity is fun to do in winter time, but you can do it any time. Pick a tree in a somewhat secluded spot. In the afternoon, decorate the tree with edible treats for animals. You could use fruit (pieces of apple, pear, or banana; grapes), nuts, bread smeared with peanut butter, vegetables, chunks of cheese, or anything else you think animals would enjoy. After you've finished, rake the ground around the tree until it is smooth.

Come back the next morning to see what treats were eaten and what tracks were left. If you can find an adult who will come with you, you can visit your tree at night and see the animals that come there.

UNDERSTANDING YOUR PET

262

If you have a dog, cat, or other pets, listen to them and watch them to see how they communicate with you and other animals.

What You'll Need: Notebook, pen, markers

Watch your pet's eyes, ears, tails, paws, and fur. And watch their whole bodies. Try to figure out what they "say" by using their bodies. Does your dog or cat ever run back and forth between you and her food bowl? Or between you and the door? ("Lemme outta here!") Does your pet roll over and look at you to let you know she wants a tummy rub?

Animals also use their voices in more ways than you might think. How many different barks does your dog have, and what do they all mean? He probably has one bark for "Someone's at the door!" and another bark for "Hey, you stepped on my paw!" He probably also growls, whines, and makes other sounds. Each sound means he's trying to communicate with you or another animal. It's the same with cats. They may have one meow to say, "Feed me!" and another to say, "Can I come in now?"

Try making a pet dictionary where you record all the different ways your pets communicate, and what you think each thing means. You could draw pictures of what your pets look like when they're "saying" different things. The more you pay attention to your pets, the better you'll understand them.

PROTECTIVE MOTHERS

Just like a human baby, a newborn animal is small and vulnerable and needs to be protected in the wild. Some animals—called marsupials—keep their young in a small pouch in front of their belly. Female kangaroos and koalas protect their babies this way. A mother crocodile takes a different approach: She carries her young in her mouth to keep them safe from harm!

263 COULD YOU BE A SQUIRREL?

Squirrels bury nuts in the fall, and dig them up to eat when food is scarce in winter. Burying the nuts is easy enough. But what about finding them?

What You'll Need: Peanuts

Squirrels can be found just about everywhere in the world. There are even real "flying" squirrels that glide from tree to tree. Try your hand at being a squirrel. Bury (or hide) 20 peanuts in the shell in 20 different places around your house. Wait a week, then see if you can find them all. Squirrels use their noses to find their buried treasures, but you'll have to use your memory! If you like, try your luck outside—but don't be surprised if a squirrel finds your secret stash before you do!

FLEAS BE GONE! 264

If you have a cat or a dog, you're probably familiar with fleas. Making an herbal flea collar is a natural way to help keep these pests away from your pet... and you!

What You'll Need: Bandanna, olive oil, oil of pennyroyal (available at an herb store, natural foods grocery, or pharmacy)

If you have a small dog or a cat, you can make a flea collar from a bandanna. Soak the bandanna in a mixture of ¼ cup olive oil and three drops of oil of pennyroyal. Let the bandanna dry, then tie it on your pet. Make sure the bandanna is big enough and tie it loosely so that it doesn't hurt your pet. After the bandanna is tied, there should be room for you to put three of your fingers between your pet's neck and the bandanna. If you have a larger dog, you can make a collar from a strip of cloth that is six inches longer than the measurement around your dog's neck.

A BASKET FOR BOWSER

265

Cats, dogs, and other furry pets will enjoy this fresh grass basket—any time of year.

What You'll Need: Herb or grass seeds or seedlings, basket without a handle, plastic trash bag, scissors, vermiculite and potting soil, plastic wrap

Cats love to munch on catnip and other good-smelling herbs. Dogs—especially dogs who live in city apartments—will enjoy frolicking with their own little patch of grass. And other pets such as hamsters, guinea pigs, and—of course—rabbits also enjoy fresh greens. Find out what kind of "salad" your pet would enjoy. Then get seeds or seedlings for those plants. Line the basket with plastic and poke a few small holes in the bottom for drainage. Put in a half-and-half mix of vermiculite and potting soil. Either plant the seedlings, or sprinkle the seeds on the soil. Water well. If you're starting from seeds, put plastic wrap over them. Put the basket in a warm sunny spot indoors. Keep it watered.

When the plants have grown to fill the basket, give your pets a present! If you keep the basket in a place where it gets light and keep it watered, the plants will keep growing to replace what your pets eat.

ALL ABOUT ANIMALS

266

One of the best ways to learn about animals is to read about them. Learn the characteristics and habits of a small, medium, or large mammal.

What You'll Need: One or more animal reference books, paper, pen

Go to a pet store, an animal shelter, or the zoo and look at the mammals they have: mice, cats, giraffes. You'll probably find that there's one kind of animal that's your favorite. Ask questions to learn about your favorite animal: What kind of home does it need? What does it eat? How does it play?

Check out a library book about the animal, read it, and then write a story about all you learned. Remember, the important thing is to have fun getting to know this very special little part of nature.

FOR THE BIRDS

Thanks to the work of conservationists early in the 20th century, all migrating songbirds are protected from harm by Federal law. Yet many are still in danger from loss of habitat, pollution, and even your neighborhood cats. (A single cat can kill dozens of birds each year!) In this chapter you will learn how you can help birds with bird feeders and birdbaths. Use these activities to create a backyard wildlife sanctuary!

267 LOOK AT THAT BEAK!

And those feet, too! Learn how birds use their beak and feet to help them survive in the wild.

What You'll Need: Field guide to birds, poster board, markers

One of the easiest ways to identify different birds is by looking at their beaks. Some have sharp beaks for pecking. Others have long, wide, flat, or curved beaks. How does each bird's beak help it get food? (A pelican's beak, for example, expands to hold the fish it catches.) Now think about birds' feet. Some have powerful feet with claws, called "talons." Other feet, like a duck's webbed feet, are designed to help birds swim. How does a bird's feet help it move around in its habitat?

Look through a field guide to birds and pay special attention to birds' beaks and feet. Then make a chart showing the beaks and feet of different birds, and telling how they help the birds survive.

SIMPLE BIRDHOUSES

268

Put some of these birdhouses out in the spring and see what kinds of birds will set up housekeeping!

What You'll Need: Gourd, carving knife, string, drill, ¼-inch dowel (optional), craft glue (optional), plastic flower pot, flower pot base, decorations

Since these houses can't be opened and cleaned easily, they are both one-season houses. You'll need an adult to help you make these birdhouses.

The easiest birdhouse to make is a gourd house. Buy or grow gourds that are at least four inches across, with a long neck. Dry out the gourd, cut a one-inch hole in the round part, and hang it up by the neck. You can also add a perch. Have an adult drill a ¼-inch hole under the larger hole. Then cut a two-inch length of dowel and insert in the small hole. Glue in place.

Another easy house begins with a plastic flower pot. First, run some string through the holes on the bottom. Cut a one-inch hole in the side of the pot. Turn it over; glue it to a flower pot base that is larger than the mouth of the flowerpot. Hang it up by the string. If you'd like, you can decorate it with dried flowers, popsicle sticks, or pine cones.

HOW TO "COLLECT" BIRDS

269

Collect birds without even catching them!

What You'll Need: Notebook, pen, field guide to birds, local bird checklist from Audubon Society (optional)

Seasoned bird-watchers—or "birders" as they call themselves—often keep a "life list" of all the birds they have seen. Start a bird collection with your own life list. Begin with a small notebook or blank book that you can carry around. Reserve the first few pages for a running list of all the different birds you see. Use field guides and local bird checklists to help you identify birds in your area. Each time you add a bird to your list, make a page for that bird. Draw its picture using the field guide to help you. Note where you saw the bird, what time of year, and what the bird was doing. Describe its song. Write down some interesting facts about the bird. Each time you see that bird again you can add more information to the page.

270

IT'S OFFICIAL

There's a lot to learn about your state—including your state bird.

What You'll Need: Field guide to birds

Find out what your official state bird is from the list below. Why do you think that bird was selected? Which bird is the state bird for seven states? Learn about your state bird from a field guide to birds. Then, whenever you're out hiking, watch for your bird. Can you find any other state birds where you live?

Alabama Yellowhammer	**Montana** Western meadowlark
Alaska Willow ptarmigan	**Nebraska** Western meadowlark
Arizona Cactus wren	**Nevada** Mountain bluebird
Arkansas Mockingbird	**New Hampshire** Purple finch
California California valley quail	**New Jersey** Eastern goldfinch
Colorado Lark bunting	**New Mexico** Roadrunner
Connecticut American robin	**New York** Bluebird
Delaware Blue hen chicken	**North Carolina** Cardinal
District of Columbia Wood thrush	**North Dakota** Western meadowlark
Florida Mockingbird	**Ohio** Cardinal
Georgia Brown thrasher	**Oklahoma** Scissor-tailed flycatcher
Hawaii Hawaiian goose	**Oregon** Western meadowlark
Idaho Mountain bluebird	**Pennsylvania** Ruffed grouse
Illinois Cardinal	**Rhode Island** Rhode Island red
Indiana Cardinal	**South Carolina** Carolina wren
Iowa Eastern goldfinch	**South Dakota** Chinese ring-necked pheasant
Kansas Western meadowlark	**Tennessee** Mockingbird
Kentucky Cardinal	**Texas** Mockingbird
Louisiana Eastern brown pelican	**Utah** Seagull
Maine Chickadee	**Vermont** Hermit thrush
Maryland Baltimore oriole	**Virginia** Cardinal
Massachusetts Chickadee	**Washington** Willow goldfinch
Michigan Robin	**West Virginia** Cardinal
Minnesota Common loon	**Wisconsin** Robin
Mississippi Mockingbird	**Wyoming** Meadowlark
Missouri Bluebird	

OWL EYES

271

Can an owl really see better than you at night? We'll shed some light on night vision.

What You'll Need: Binoculars

When it's almost dark, go outside and try your best to see. (Go to an area where there are no outdoor lights.) Pay attention to how much you can see: the outline of a tree or house? a cat moving? Now, look through binoculars. Can you see more?

You can see better through binoculars because they take in more light than your eyes can. But even with binoculars, you're no match for an owl. Owls' eyes take in about 100 times more light than yours, so they can see quite well at night.

FAVORITE FOODS

272

Different kinds of birds have very different ideas about what makes a nice meal. See which birds eat which foods.

What You'll Need: Pie plates, several kinds of bird food (birdseed, sunflower seeds, oats, bread crumbs), paper, pen

First, gather several different kinds of bird food, including birdseed, sunflower seeds, oats, bread crumbs, and anything else you can think of. Put each kind of food in a separate pie pan, then put all the pie pans outside, a few feet apart. Watch from a distance or from inside to see which kinds of birds eat which foods. Keep a record of this.

Try putting some of the pie pans on the ground, and some up high in bird feeders or trees, and watch what happens. Then, switch the pie pans around. Put the ones that were on the ground up high. What do you discover? You'll probably see that some birds prefer to eat on the ground, while others only eat in the trees. Birds may ignore even their favorite food if it's in the wrong place! If you try this activity at different times of the year, you may see different kinds of birds.

HUMMINGBIRD FEEDER

273

Whip up some special food for these special birds.

What You'll Need: Plastic bottle, scissors, sugar, water, pot, craft glue, decorative flowers, string

Hummingbirds can hover, fly backwards, and even fly upside down. They flap their wings up to 78 times per second. All that flapping burns up the calories, so hummingbirds have to eat half their weight in food every day. Of course, some only weigh about one-tenth of an ounce.

It should come as no surprise that hummingbirds don't eat the same things as other birds. They need high-energy foods, and one of their favorite foods is nectar collected from red flowers. They also love sugar syrup. Here's how to make a hummingbird feeder:

Wash a large, clear plastic soda bottle and remove the label. About one-fourth of the way from the bottom of the bottle, cut a square hole that is about one inch on each side. Make a crease in the front of the bottle, just above the hole.

With an adult's help, boil ½ cup of sugar and 2 cups of water to make a syrup. Let the syrup cool. Use your finger to cover the hole in the bottle, and pour in the syrup. Put the lid on the bottle. Glue red plastic flowers on the bottle, especially near the hole. Tie a string around the top of the bottle, and use it to hang the feeder.

GROW A BIRD FEEDER

274

Sunflowers are natural bird feeders—they grow tall, and offer seeds.

What You'll Need: Sunflower seeds, a garden plot, tall stakes, hammer, string

To grow sunflowers, plant some seeds in a sunny place. Be sure to plant sunflowers in a place where they can be reached with a hose, because they'll need lots of water. You won't believe how fast sunflowers grow, and how big and tall they get! When they start to grow tall, have an adult help you hammer a stake in the ground next to each sunflower stalk. Use string to tie the stake to the stalk in several places. Don't forget to water your sunflowers often. In a few months they'll make big yellow flowers. At the center of each flower will be a large cluster of seeds. When the seeds are ready to eat, the birds will know.

WINTER BIRD TREATS

275

When the weather gets cold, give winter birds a much needed treat.

What You'll Need: Ground suet (found at meat counters in grocery stores), two pans, bowl, water, strainer, birdseed, aluminum foil, disposable plastic food storage containers, mesh onion sack, peanut butter, shortening, whole wheat flour, cornmeal

To make suet cakes: Put two pounds of ground suet in a large pan and add two quarts of water. Simmer until all the fat is melted. Strain into a bowl and let it cool, then put in the refrigerator until the fat is hard. Remove the hardened fat and put into a small pan. Melt it over low heat. Add three or four cups of birdseed. Make molds by shaping two layers of aluminum foil over the outside of a plastic food container. Pour the suet-birdseed mix into the molds. (Two pounds of suet will make three 4-inch by 6-inch cakes.) You can put the cakes on a platform feeder out of reach of squirrels or hang them in a mesh onion sack.

To make bird treats: Mix two parts of peanut butter with one part each of shortening, whole wheat flour, cornmeal, and birdseed. Mix in a large bowl. Roll the mixture into balls and put in a feeder.

SUET BELL

276

All types of birds will love this tasty "dinner bell."

What You'll Need: Birdseed; dried fruit; bread crumbs; suet, lard, or fat drippings; yogurt container; string

First, gather birdseed, bread crumbs, and dried fruit. These ingredients are the "filler" for this project. Next, collect some suet, lard, or drippings from a roast or bacon. (You'll need about ½ pound of suet for every pound of filler.) Ask an adult to melt the suet in a saucepan and mix in the filler. Let the mixture cool a little.

Poke a small hole in the bottom of a yogurt container. Tie a knot in a length of string and pull the string about halfway through the hole. Make sure there are several inches of string inside the container and several inches outside. Have an adult pour the suet and filler mixture into the yogurt container. Leave it there overnight to harden. Carefully remove the yogurt container. Use the string to hang the suet bell in a tree where birds gather.

BIRDBATH

277

Water is often in short supply in the wild. Give some feathered friends a hand by providing precious water.

What You'll Need: Flat pan, rock, PVC pipe (six inches wide), rope (¼-inch thick), brick, garbage can lid

Bird feeders will attract many birds to your backyard, but water will attract even more, especially on dry summer days or when water supplies freeze over in winter. For a simple birdbath, just lay a shallow pan of water on the ground. You can put a rock in the pan to keep it from getting knocked over.

For a more permanent birdbath: With help from an adult, cut a four-foot length of six-inch diameter PVC pipe. Sink it about two feet into the ground. Next, cut a three foot length of ¼-inch rope. Tie one end of the rope to a heavy rock or brick. Tie the other end to the handle of a garbage can lid. Drop the rock or brick down the pipe. It should hang about halfway down. The weight of the hanging brick holds the garbage can lid in place upside-down. Fill the lid with water. To clean, simply lift the lid out and wash it.

THE PINE CONE CAFÉ

278

A pine cone makes a natural "snack shop" for birds. Here's how to make a pine cone bird feeder.

What You'll Need: Large pine cone, string, peanut butter, birdseed

Tie a string from the top of a pine cone. Then smear lots of peanut butter all over the cone. Next roll the cone in birdseed so the seeds stick in the peanut butter. It may not make *your* mouth water, but to birds, it's a treat. Hang the pine cone from a branch, and birds will begin stopping by for a snack.

BUILD A BIRD'S NEST

279

Birds spend lots of time collecting materials to make a cozy nest.

What You'll Need: Nature and human-made materials, modeling clay

In addition to twigs and leaves, birds like to use bits of string, yarn, lint, and other human-made materials to build and furnish their homes. Take a walk outside and pretend that you are a bird that needs to make a nest. See what building materials you can find. Look for natural materials like leaves and twigs, and also for human-made materials.

When you get back home, shape some modeling clay into a bird's nest. Line the inside and outside of the nest with the things you collected, until you come up with the perfect bird home. This makes a great piece of art for your home.

BE A BIRD'S HELPER

280

In the springtime, birds are on the lookout for nesting material. Here's how to give them a helping hand.

What You'll Need: String, scissors, short strips of old rags, other nest lining

You can encourage birds to nest in your area if you provide them with natural nesting materials, or artificial materials that birds will accept as well as the natural ones. Cut pieces of string into lengths no longer than three inches (or birds can get tangled in it). Short, narrow strips of rag are also useful to birds. Feathers from an old feather pillow are often acceptable as nest lining. If your family discards lawn clippings, save some to dry and give to the birds.

String, rags, and dried grass can be laid out on the ground or on branches of shrubs for birds to pick up. Hang a used berry basket up on a tree limb and fill it with bits of lint or with small feathers.

If you have swallows in your yard, try this trick: In the spring when the swallows first return, go outdoors in an area where you've seen swallows and hold a fluffy white feather in your fingertips as high as you can. The swallows will dive at the feather until one gets brave enough to snatch it from your fingers and take it home to its nest.

EXAMINE A BIRD FEATHER

281

Take a closer look at the complex structure of feathers. It will give you great information to add to your bird notebook.

What You'll Need: Feathers, gloves, magnifying glass, bird notebook (see page 179)

Next time you find bird feathers outdoors take some time for a closer look. (Some bird feathers carry disease, so be careful to wear gloves when you handle them.) If you keep a bird notebook, you can add this information to your notes. Most feathers you find will have a hollow *quill* running down the center. Coming out of both sides of the quill are *barbs*. Look at them carefully with your magnifying glass. Notice the small, hooklike *barbules* that make the barbs stick together.

Feathers come in three basic types: *Down feathers* have no quill to speak of. The barbs are soft, and the barbules do not stick together. *Body* (or contour) *feathers,* have downy barbs at the base for insulation, while the upper part forms a flat, windproof layer. *Flight feathers* have no downy parts at all. They are long and stiff, and form the shape of the wings. Draw your findings in your notebook. Using the color and the size of the feather, see if you can figure out what bird it came from. When you are done looking at the feather, put it back where you found it. Laws that protect our nation's birds also protect bird parts. Some feathers can be collected by permit only.

WHAT A BEAK!

The South American swordbill is a bird whose bill is as long as its head and body put together! This bird lives in the South American rain forest, and he needs his long beak to gather his food, the nectar from the long, tube-shaped flowers of the passiflora plant. The bird's bill can be as long as four full inches.

NATURE'S PEN

282

You may find it hard to believe, but 200 years ago, quill pens were the most popular way to write. Make your own pen from a bird feather.

What You'll Need: Large feather, soap, water, scissors, pin, ink

Buy a feather at a crafts store. It should have a stout quill and be about 10 inches long. Soak the feather in warm soapy water for several minutes. Then rinse the feather and let it dry. Use a scissors to trim off the bottom two inches of feather from both sides of the quill. Then cut the end of the quill to a point. Use a straight pin to gently clean out the inside of the quill. Be very careful not to crack or break the quill. Finally, ask an adult to cut a small slit in the point of the quill.

To use your quill pen, dip the end in ink. (The hollow quill will hold a little ink.) Blot extra ink on a piece of old newspaper before you write. To write with a quill pen, you need to hold it at an angle. It takes a little practice, but you'll get the hang of it!

FEATHER PAINTING

283

Feathers are good for the inside of pillows, to tickle your friend's nose, and as great painting tools!

What You'll Need: Newspaper, three feathers (available at a crafts store), poster paints, India ink, clean foam meat trays, drawing paper, scissors or knife

Cover your work surface with newspaper. Pour some paints in a clean foam tray, then pour a bit of ink in a second tray. Now paint a picture on your paper using a different part of each feather: the feather tip, the feather web, and the quill end.

Dip the tip and web in the paint and use them to create soft, sweeping lines. Dip the quill end in the ink to create sharp lines, dots, and points.

WINTER DELIGHT

284

When it gets cold, life is rough for birds. Next time it snows, turn a snowman into a bird's best friend!

What You'll Need: Snow, bird treats

In winter, when many of the things that birds like to eat are covered with snow, the birds could use your help. Make a snowman (or snow person) and decorate it with things birds like to eat. That includes birdseed and fruit. Your snow creation is likely to have lots of feathered friends.

You can make several snow people—or even a whole snow family! Use different kinds of food and see if you attract a variety of birds. You may also attract squirrels, rabbits, and other types of backyard wildlife.

1 BIRD, 2 BIRDS, 3 BIRDS

285

Every year around Christmastime, birdwatchers all over the country get together for a special event. Join the Chrismas Bird Count.

You'll learn a lot about birds by spending a day with other people who care about them. The Christmas Bird Count is sponsored by the Audubon Society, an organization of people who are interested in birds. The purpose of the count is to find out how many birds there are, and what kinds of birds.

Here's how it works: People form groups, and each group counts birds in a certain area on a certain day. The groups count how many birds there are of each kind. Then, all the groups send their counts to the Audubon Society, who adds everything up to get the big picture. If you'd like to be part of the Christmas Bird Count, call a nature center or bird-watching club in your area for information. They can help you become part of a group.

'TIS THE SEASON

286

Decorate a neighborhood tree with these wonderful holiday ornaments for the birds.

What You'll Need: Cookie cutters, bread, yarn, peanut butter, birdseed

To make holiday tree ornaments that birds will enjoy, use cookie cutters to cut shapes out of bread. Next, poke a piece of yarn through each shape. Spread peanut butter on the shapes, and press seeds into the peanut butter. Hang the shapes from an outdoor tree with the yarn, and watch the birds flock around.

DID YOU CALL ME?

287

Just like people from different parts of the world, birds speak a "foreign" language. Learn to identify and imitate birdcalls.

What You'll Need: Field guide to birds

Go to an area where there are lots of birds and eavesdrop on their conversations. Listen and look at the same time, and begin to learn which sounds are made by which birds. If you know how, you can actually get birds to come close to you so you can watch and listen to them. One way is to buy a birdcall at a nature store. Or, try this method: Open your lips but keep your teeth together. Put your tongue lightly against the back of your teeth, and blow out. Stand very still while you do this, so the birds notice the sound, but don't notice you.

Listen to birds and try to imitate their sounds. The better your imitation is, the more interested the birds will be. Pay close attention to what the birds look like, so you can try to find them later in a field guide.

Some of the easiest birds to imitate are the whippoorwill, the bobwhite, and the chickadee. Owls are fun to imitate, too, although it's not always as simple as "who?" or "hoot!" If you hear a deep, loud hoot, you're probably hearing a Great Horned Owl, which lives all over North America. If you hear eight hoots in a row, you probably are hearing the Barred Owl. (It's nicknamed the "Eight Hooter.") If you hear a loud noise that sounds like a monkey, but you don't live in the jungle, you're probably hearing another type of call of the Barred Owl.

WHERE ARE YOU HEADED?

288

Here's an easy way to study birds' migration routes.

What You'll Need: Reference book, globe or world map, rubber cement, different colored yarn

Migratory birds fly thousands of miles every year. At the library, check out a book about migratory birds. See if your home is on the migration path of any birds. (If it is, watch for them at the times of the year when they migrate.) Then, on a globe or world map, mark the migration paths of some birds. Use rubber cement or other temporary adhesive to attach a piece of yarn to each bird's starting place. Then attach the other end of the yarn to the bird's summer home. Use different colors of yarn for different birds.

ROBIN'S EGG TREATS

289

Robin Redbreast's eggs don't taste like jellybeans, but these "eggs" do!

What You'll Need: 1⅓ cups flaked coconut; cookie sheets; 3 bowls; 1 cup butter, softened; ½ cup sugar; 1 egg; ½ teaspoon lemon extract; 2 cups all-purpose flour; ½ teaspoon salt; ½ teaspoon orange peel; shortening; 1 cup small jellybeans

Be sure to have an adult help you with this project. Preheat oven to 300°F. Spread coconut on ungreased cookie sheet. Bake in oven for about 25 minutes or until coconut begins to brown; stir occasionally. Put toasted coconut in bowl.

Increase oven temperature to 350°F. Beat butter and sugar in a large bowl until fluffy. Add egg and lemon extract; beat until smooth. Combine flour, salt, and orange peel in a medium bowl. Add flour mixture to butter mixture; blend.

Separate dough into 36 small balls; roll each ball in toasted coconut until completely covered. Place each dough ball 2 inches apart on greased cookie sheets. Using your thumb, make a dent in the center of each ball.

Bake 12 to 14 minutes or until coconut is golden brown. Remove to wire racks and cool completely. Put jellybean "eggs" in the indentations of cooled cookies. Makes 3 dozen treats.

FLIGHTLESS BIRDS

All birds have feathers, but not all birds can fly. Because of this, they have developed other ways of escaping their enemies. Penguins use their flipperlike wings to help them "fly" as they swim at great speed through water. Larger birds—like the emu and ostrich—have strong legs and can run very fast. (Ostriches can run at speeds of more than 35 miles per hour!)

290 CURIOUS AS A BIRD?

Learn about the interesting habits and traits of birds. Then create your own bird book.

What You'll Need: Reference book about birds, index cards, pen, markers, stapler

From the tiny hummingbird to the giant ostrich, there are a lot of different kinds of birds in the world. And they all have different habitats. Seagulls and pelicans live along water shores. Penguins live in cold, arctic regions. You can find many strange and colorful types of birds (like the toucan) in rain forests and tropical islands. Even large cities can be home to sparrows, pigeons, doves, and many other varieties of birds. What kind of birds live near you?

Get some books on birds out of the library, study them, and pick out your favorite variety of bird. Afterwards, write a mini-book on a day in the life of this bird.

Use an index card for each page of your book. Start by drawing a cover on the first index card (put your name as the author). Then write an interesting fact about the bird on each card. Don't forget to leave room for illustrations; include pictures of the bird's shape, nest, and habitat. What does your bird eat? Is it most active during the day or at night? Where does it live? When all of your pages are done, staple them together.

WATER, WATER, EVERYWHERE

Nothing can live without water, so streams, seashores, ponds, lakes, and other bodies of water attract a huge variety of fish and other marine life. Wetlands of all kinds are terrific places to see nature. But animals aren't all you should notice. Many plants have developed interesting adaptations to live in wetlands or near seashores. This chapter has plenty of crafts and activities to help you understand water. Have fun in the water, but always be safe.

291 BOTTLE IT!

Now you can watch the waves without having to leave your home when you make a sea-in-a-bottle.

What You'll Need: Clear plastic bottle with top, water, blue food coloring, mineral oil

Many people are soothed by the sight and sound of ocean waves. Here's how to really make waves! Fill a large plastic bottle ⅔ full of water. Add blue food coloring to the water and mix it up. Fill the rest of the bottle with mineral oil, so there's no room for air. Then put the top on the bottle.

Lay the bottle on its side. Watch as the mineral oil floats to the top. To make waves in your sea, tilt the bottle back and forth. You can imagine you're at the beach or sailing on the ocean.

IS THAT ALL THERE IS?

292

Why is it so important to keep rivers and lakes clean? Make a chart showing how precious our freshwater supply really is.

What You'll Need: Poster board, markers

You can do this activity with a group of friends. Get a big piece of poster board and draw 100 circles, all the same size. (You can trace around a quarter or a very small cup. Just make sure there's room on your poster board for 100 circles, with some room left over.) Now color 97 of the circles all the same color. These circles will stand for all the saltwater on Earth. Next, color two circles another color. These two circles will stand for all the frozen water on Earth.

How many circles are left? That's right, only one. That circle stands for all the freshwater on Earth. Color it a third color. That one circle has to provide all the water humans need for drinking, watering crops, and everything else.

Think of a title for your poster. Also, somewhere on the poster, make a key to explain what the chart means. See if you can put up your chart at a library or school.

WATER MAGNIFIER

293

One well known quality of water is that it makes things wet! But did you know that water also makes things look larger than they really are?

What You'll Need: Piece of glass or plastic, newspaper, crayon, eyedropper, water

Get a small piece of clear glass or plastic. (A microscope slide is ideal.) Always be careful when handling glass. Put the slide on top of a piece of newspaper that has small print on it. Now use a crayon to draw a small circle on the slide. Look closely at the print that is within the circle.

With an eyedropper, carefully put a drop of water in the circle. Now look at the print again. Does it look larger? This is because the water drop bends rays of light, magnifying the image.

THIRSTY?

294

In very hot or very cold weather, wild animals may have trouble finding enough water to drink. Quench their thirst with an animal "drinking fountain."

What You'll Need: Plastic milk jug, large shallow container, tape, water

In hot weather, the usual sources of water may evaporate or run dry. In cold weather, these same water sources may freeze. Help the animals by putting water out for them.

If the wildlife in your area consists of small animals (such as squirrels, chipmunks, skunks, rabbits, and raccoons), you can make a small water basin out of a plastic milk jug with the top cut off. Put tape around the rim to cover the sharp edge. Make sure the container is shallow enough that these small critters can drink out of it. Put a few rocks in the bottom of the container so the animals don't accidentally knock it over. If predators (such as coyotes or wild cats) live nearby, put the water near trees, so small animals have an escape route if danger appears. If larger animals (such as deer) live in your area, you'll want to use a larger container. A galvanized tub from a hardware store works well.

In summer, refill containers often to offset evaporation. In winter, go out every morning. If ice has formed in the container, break it up and add more water if needed. *Remember:* Water in small, shallow containers will freeze more quickly than water in large, deep containers. If water is scarce, your "drinking fountains" will attract many animals. At dawn and dusk, stand back at a safe distance and watch them.

ALL KINDS OF WATER

295

Water doesn't just come in one shape. It has three different states, depending on its temperature.

What You'll Need: Ice, pan

To see all three states, put some ice in a pan. With adult help, put the pan on the stove and turn on the heat. First the ice will begin turning to liquid, then the liquid will begin turning to steam. Ice and snow melt at 32°F (0°C) and water turns into steam at 212°F (100°C).

IT'S A TENSE SITUATION

296

How high can you fill a glass with water? This experiment will demonstrate the power of surface tension.

What You'll Need: Glass, water, eyedropper

Fill a glass to the very top with water. Then use an eyedropper to add water, very gently, one drop at a time. You'll see that you can add drops until the water level is actually *above* the rim of the glass! How is this possible?

Here's the explanation: The water molecules are attracted to one another, but not to air molecules. So, as long as they possibly can, the water molecules will stick together in the glass, rather than falling over the edge of the glass. This tendency of water molecules to stick together is called "surface tension." A surface tension gives water the appearance of having a "skin" across the top of the glass. This is also why small droplets of water stay in a round shape rather than spreading out in all directions.

LIQUID LAYERS

297

We all know that rocks are heavier than feathers. But which is lighter—water or oil? See which liquid is the heavyweight champion.

What You'll Need: Large clear jar with a tight-fitting lid, water, food coloring, vegetable oil

Put some water in your jar and color it with food coloring. Now slowly pour in some vegetable oil. Put the lid on the jar and shake it. Let the liquids settle. What happens? The word "density" refers to how closely packed the molecules are. The higher the density, the heavier it is. Which liquid has the highest density? Frozen water is less dense than its liquid form. That is why ice floats on top of water! The density of our bodies is very close to that of water—or else we wouldn't be able to float in a swimming pool.

LIQUID MELODIES

298

Have you ever noticed all the different sounds that water makes? Learn how to make music with water.

What You'll Need: Bottles, jars, or drinking glasses of different sizes, water, spoon or stick

Go around your house and yard, and see how many different sounds you can make with water. Try the faucets, from barely on to full blast. Listen to the shower, the hose, the sprinkler. Drop ice cubes into a glass of water. Any other ideas? Now think of water sounds in nature: a soft rain, a hard rain, waves, a waterfall. It's a regular symphony, isn't it?

Speaking of a symphony, here's one way to make music with water. Gather several glass bottles, jars, and/or drinking glasses of different shapes and sizes. (Always be careful when handling glass.) Put water in them—a little water or a lot. Use a spoon or a small stick to tap the containers, and see what different notes they make. Can you arrange the containers from lowest note to highest note? Can you change the level of water in the containers to create new notes? How about making up a song to play on your water instruments?

I'M M-E-L-T-I-N-G!

299

Watch time practically stand still when you make an ice cube melt in slow motion.

What You'll Need: Drinking glass, vegetable oil, ice cube

Fill a drinking glass with vegetable oil. Now drop an ice cube into the oil. As the ice melts, you will be able to see the droplets form and fall in slow motion. The droplets fall this way because water has a higher density than oil.

HELLO DOWN THERE!

300

Have you ever looked at the surface of a pond or stream and wished you could see what was going on down there? With this aquascope, now you can.

What You'll Need: Half-gallon milk carton, scissors, plastic wrap, large rubber band, heavy tape

Start with an empty half-gallon milk carton. Cut the bottom and top off the carton. Stretch clear plastic wrap over one end of the carton. Use a big rubber band to hold it in place tight, or use heavy tape. You just made your own aquascope.

Now head for that pond or stream. If the water is deep, have an adult along with you. Hold the plastic-covered end of your aquascope just under the surface of the water, and look through the other end. What's going on down there? Be careful not to harm any of the wildlife.

PRESTO CHANGE-O!

301

Seawater contains salt, which makes it unfit to drink. Here's how can you change saltwater to freshwater.

What You'll Need: Pot, salt, aluminum foil, bowl

Fill a pot with water. Now put in some salt. This is your "seawater." Use aluminum foil to make a "tent" that covers the pot and slopes over a wide, shallow bowl. With adult help, bring the water to a boil.

As the water boils and turns to steam, the steam will condense on the foil and drip into the bowl. Let most of the water move from the pot to the bowl. Then let the water cool.

Look at the water in the bowl and taste it. How is it different from the water in the pot? What happened to the salt? This method of making freshwater is called "distillation," and is used to help provide water to areas where only seawater is available.

"READ" A CREEK

302

You can learn a lot about a creek or stream—if you know where to look!

If there is a creek or stream near where you live, spend some time walking along its banks. I the water is deep, have an adult go along with you. Pay close attention to the different kinds of plants and animals that live in the water and on the banks.

Look closely at the current. Is it the same everywhere, or is it faster in some places and slower in others? Can you think of reasons for the differences? (For one thing, the current is swifter where the water is shallow, and slower where the water is deep.) What about the surface of the water? Is it smooth in some places and choppy in others? A small area of choppy water might mean there is a rock or large log just under the surface.

Is the water level in the creek higher or lower than normal? You can tell by looking at the banks. If there is bare, damp soil along the banks, the creek is lower than normal. If you see green land plants or trees grow ing out of the water, the creek is higher than normal. Can you tell why the creek flows where it does? Does it go around obstacles, such as large rocks?

JUST PASSING THROUGH

303

It's amazing all the things that travel down the watery highway of a creek!

What You'll Need: Wire coat hanger or piece of strong wire, screen or mesh, duct tape

Bend a wire coat hanger into a rough circle. Take a piece of old screen, and bend it around the coat hanger. (Be careful not to stick yourself with the screen. You may want to wear work gloves or gardening gloves while doing this.) Use duct tape to hold the screen in place.

Now go to a creek or stream with an adult. Put your screen into the current and hold it there for a few minutes. Take out the screen and see what the current has carried onto it. You might find seeds that will land on the creek's bank and grow into plants. Or, you might find water animals such as insects, minnows, or crayfish. (Put them back in the creek right away, so they stay alive.) You might even find something somebody lost a long way upstream.

ICE HANGINGS

304

When the weather turns cold, you can make these temporary-but-beautiful natural decorations.

What You'll Need: Pie plate, water, yarn, nature objects (flowers, berries, evergreen sprigs)

Fill a pie pan with water and line the edge with yarn, making sure the yarn is submerged in the water. Leave the ends of the yarn loose, so you can hang up your project when it's finished.

Next, arrange your objects in the center of the pan. You can use fresh or dried flowers, greenery, berries, or anything you like. If the temperature outside is below freezing, set your plate outdoors. Or you can place it in the freezer. Wait until the yarn and flowers are frozen completely into the ice before removing.

Once it is frozen, you can remove the ice circle from the pan. (Dip the bottom of the pan in warm water if you need help removing it.) Now hang it up outdoors on a tree, post, or anywhere its beauty can be seen. Watch your creation sparkle in the sun. As long as the temperatures stay below freezing, your ice hanging won't melt away.

BE AN EXPLORER

305

Discover your own uncharted territory! Visit a river, stream, lake, pond, or tide pool.

What You'll Need: Notebook, pen

In 1804–1806, Meriwether Lewis and William Clark were the first European-Americans to travel across what is now the western United States. They kept journals full of notes and drawings to tell the rest of the world about all the strange, new things they saw: plants, animals, mountains, and much more.

With an adult, visit a body of water near your home. Imagine that you are an explorer. Look closely at the plants, animals, rocks, and other natural elements. Tell about them in a journal. Finally, make a map of the area for explorers who will follow in your footsteps. Don't forget that explorers may find all kinds of surprises. Meriwether Lewis met a grizzly bear one day, and had to jump into a river to escape!

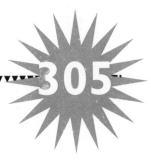

306 UNDERWATER NIGHT LIFE

Some water-dwellers are more active at night than during the day. Here's how to get a close-up look at these creatures of the night.

What You'll Need: Strong flashlight, plastic bags, tape, rope or string

Have an adult go along with you for this project. At night, go down to a dock or a similar place where you can look down into water at least a few feet deep. You could also go out on a pond in a boat. Whether on a dock or a boat, always put on a life vest for safety.

Seal a flashlight into a plastic, zipper-type bag. Roll the bag around the flashlight, then seal it in a second bag. Tape the edges for a watertight seal. Tie a light rope or heavy string to the flashlight, turn it on, and lower it down into the water. Now wait patiently. Soon the light will attract curious creatures. See what kinds of fish and other creatures are active at night. Keep a nature notebook. Draw what you see and try to identify the animals. Try this in several different areas and compare. See what differences there are between different bodies of water.

DEEP FREEZE? 307

Why doesn't the ocean freeze in winter? Discover how salt can affect the properties of water.

What You'll Need: Two plastic cups, water, salt

Fill two cups halfway with water. Add some salt to one of the cups and stir it up. Now place both cups in the freezer or outside if temperatures are below freezing. Which one freezes first? You'll find that the salt in the water makes it harder to freeze. Depending on the amount of salt in it, saltwater may need to be 25 degrees colder than fresh water to freeze! This is one of the reasons why salt is used to melt ice on sidewalks and streets. It's also one of the reasons why the ocean doesn't completely freeze when the weather gets cold.

THE LIVING OCEAN

308

Oceans don't just contain saltwater. They encompass many different living things. Make a diorama of this underwater world.

What You'll Need: Book on the ocean, shoe box, markers or paint, paper, scissors, decorations

When you think of the ocean, you probably think about swimming at the beach or going for a boat ride. Those are fun things, but they're not the only ways oceans are used. Oceans are home to many unusual and delicate forms of life, like starfish, algae, seahorses, coral, anemones, and of course lots of fish. Find a book about sea life, and learn about all the different things that are found in the world's oceans. Then choose a part of the ocean and make a diorama that shows what you learned. You may want to show a coral reef, or a deep part of the ocean. What kind of animals or plants live there? On the inside bottom of a shoe box, draw or paint a blue background to represent water. You can cut and color paper fish and plants and glue them to the background. Then turn the shoe box on its side. Now make the "floor" of your ocean. You might put in sand and shells, or make plants and animals (like lobster or crab) out of clay to populate your ocean.

CHANGING SHAPES

309

Nothing in nature stays exactly the same. See how a body of water changes over time.

Visit a body of water—a creek, river, pond, or lake—about once a week. Notice how it changes. Does the water level go up and down? (If you can get permission, stick a yardstick in the mud at the edge of the water. Then you'll be able to tell exactly how much the water rises and falls.) What happens when it rains? Or when it doesn't rain for a long time? When the water level goes up, what other changes occur? Does the water get muddier? Does it change color? How are plants and animals affected?

310 WHAT'S INSIDE?

Like a pearl inside an oyster, this seashell box makes a wonderful hiding place for a small treasure.

What You'll Need: Hinged seashell, craft glue, ribbon

Shells start out as homes to sea creatures. But once the creature is gone, shells can be homes for all kinds of interesting things. If you have both halves of a hinged seashell (they're called "bivalves"), you can make it into a small box for a prized possession. Just glue a piece of ribbon or fabric to both inside halves of the shell, where they connect. The ribbon will act as a hinge so you can open and close the box. You can paint or decorate the shell—or enjoy its natural beauty!

CLAMSHELL GARDEN

311

You can find clams on the beach—or at a local fish market. Create a miniature garden out of a clamshell.

What You'll Need: Clam half-shell, small cactus, craft glue, sand, small pebbles (no larger than ⅛-inch in diameter), moss, potting soil, seeds

To make a cactus garden: Place a tiny variety of cactus inside the clamshell, using a small amount of glue to hold it in place. Fill the shell with a mixture of half sand and half a combination of tiny pebbles and moss. Dampen and place in a sunny spot. Your garden should be watered once a week. Be careful not to over-water it.

To make a seed garden: Sprinkle tiny pebbles along the bottom of the clamshell, followed by a half-inch of potting soil. Spread moss on top. Dampen and sprinkle on some seeds (grass seeds work well, or you can try alfalfa, clover, mustard seed, radish, or rye). Layer more soil over seeds and moss. Water lightly and keep it in a dark place until the seeds sprout, then move it to a sunny spot.

SEASHORE LIFE

The seashore is the part of the world where water and land meet. Fascinating forms of life live there, such as barnacles, winkles, and limpets. Barnacles are small creatures that stick themselves on surrounding rock, waiting for the tide to bring them food. Winkles are like snails; they glide over rocks, scraping food off them with their rough tongue. Limpets are tiny seashore animals that can accurately return to their homes, locating their exact hollow in the correct rock.

ART FROM THE OCEAN

312

Seaweed has interesting shapes and textures. You can preserve them by making seaweed prints.

What You'll Need: Fresh seaweed (available at fish supply stores), poster board, craft glue, decorations

It's easy to make seaweed prints! Just lay fresh seaweed on a piece of poster board. Arrange it in a nice design, then let the seaweed dry. Seaweed contains a gluelike substance that will cause it to stick to the poster board. When the seaweed is dry, check to make sure it's all stuck to the poster board. If there are loose bits of seaweed, just use a little glue to stick them down. If you like, you can paint your creation or decorate it with other things you find at a beach—like shells or pebbles.

SAND CASTING

313

You can make more out of beach sand than castles. Create unusual sculptures of plaster right on the beach!

What You'll Need: Moist beach sand, bucket, nature objects, paper cup, plaster of Paris

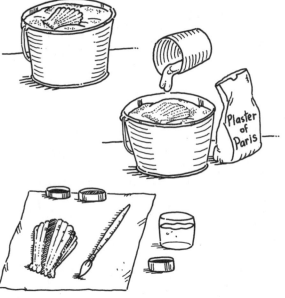

To make the mold: Gather a bucket of moist beach sand and carry it to where it won't be disturbed. Now gather some natural objects with interesting shapes, such as seashells. Be careful not to disturb nature areas. Press the objects into the sand, then remove them. The dents in the sand are molds of your object.

To make the sculpture: In a paper cup, mix plaster of Paris with water until it is just runny enough to pour. Fill your molds with plaster and leave them to dry. When they have hardened, remove your sculptures from the sand. You can paint them or may wish to leave them in their "natural" state. Always clean up any plaster left on the beach, so that it doesn't damage the habitat.

I SEE SEASHELLS

314

Turn an ordinary box into a keepsake container using seashells—the perfect gift from the sea.

What You'll Need: Shells, craft glue, shoe box

Collect seashells of all different sizes, shapes, and colors. You can also find real or artificial shells at a craftsw store. Be careful not to collect any shells with the animal still inside them. Then turn your shell collection into a work of art that also houses your favorite items. Glue your shells onto a shoe box in the shape of a picture or any design. You can even spell your name in shells on the top of the box.

THERE GOES THE BEACH!

315

Water has the power to wear down rocks and soil—even beaches. You can make a beach-in-a-pan to see how erosion happens in nature.

What You'll Need: Large rectangular pan, brick, sand, gravel, water, sponge

Set one end of your pan on a brick so the end of the pan is raised a few inches. Next, use sand and gravel to make a "beach" at the high end of the pan. (You may need to dampen the sand to make it stay in place.) Pour water into the low end of the pan until the water reaches the beach.

Now put a thick sponge in the water at the low end of the pan. Push down on the sponge to make waves in your ocean. Watch what the waves do to the beach. That's erosion!

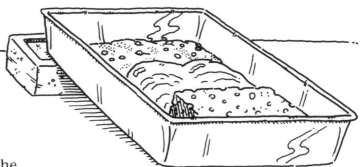

DEEP SEA LIFE

If you traveled downward in the ocean, below 330 feet, it would get darker and darker. Soon it would be as black as night. There are fish that live there, but they look quite strange. Some, like the lantern fish and the stomiatoids, have tiny glowing lights. Other fish have silvery sides that act like mirrors—and the angler fish has a projection that dangles from its head. It acts like bait, attracting other fish, which the angler fish can gobble up.

FISH PRINTS

"Gyotaku"—or fish printing—is a well-respected form of art in Japan. Make your own beautiful prints using real fish.

What You'll Need: Water-based ink or tempura paint, thin paper (real rice paper is best, but newsprint will work), fish with heavy scales, pan, brush

You can buy special inks and rice paper for your prints, or simply use newsprint and paint. Select a fish with large scales for the best prints. Lay it in a pan and wipe it clean. Using a brush, cover the fish with a very thin coat of water-based ink or paint. You can make the whole fish one color, or use different colors on the fins, make stripes—or whatever you like.

Next, lay the paper on top of the fish. Gently press the paper onto the fish, using your fingers to shape it around the curves of the fish's body. Slowly peel back the paper and look at your print. Try printing again without adding more ink. Sometimes the second print is better. You can make fishy t-shirts and bandannas if you use fabric paint instead of ink or tempera paint.

A Big Fish Story

When you think of a fish, you may think of small ones, such as a pet goldfish. Fish range in size, however, from less than ½ inch long—the dwarf goby—to 40-foot long whale sharks. In 1959, Alfred Dean went fishing by Australia, and he reeled in a white shark that actually weighed 2,664 pounds!

PUFFY FISH

3 | 7

Toilet tissue or newspaper help these fish puff up in 3-D! You can use them to make a fishy mobile.

What You'll Need: Colored tissue paper, markers, scissors, craft glue, toilet tissue or newspaper, stick, thread

Lay two pieces of tissue paper together. Draw the outline of a fish, then carefully cut the shape out of both pieces of tissue. This will be the front and back of your fish. Decorate it any way you like. You can make it look like a real fish or a funny cartoon one. Next, apply a thin line of glue along the inside edge of the front half of your fish, leaving the tail unglued. Put the two pieces of tissue together and let the glue dry. When it's dry, stuff your fish with toilet tissue or newspaper to make it puff out! Glue the tail shut. You can make a fishy mobile by tying several fish to a stick with thread.

OCEAN MOTION

Creatures in the ocean use many unusual methods to move. Fish swim by moving their bodies from side to side, but whales and dolphins move their tails up and down. Squids and octopuses shoot water out of a nozzle, forcing themselves to move along, and sea slugs creep along the bottom of the sea on a muscle called a foot.

THIS WATERY WORLD

318

About three-quarters of the Earth's surface is covered with water. Find out more when you read all about oceans or rivers.

What You'll Need: One or more books about oceans or rivers, paper, pen

Do you know the names of the world's four major oceans? (They are the Pacific, Atlantic, Indian, and Arctic.) How about the two longest rivers? (They're the Nile and the Amazon.) Before people even knew that the Earth was round, great explorers sailed across oceans and down rivers to see what they could see. Some of the most fascinating creatures in the world live in the oceans and rivers.

See if your library some books on oceans and rivers. Then compare similarities and contrast the differences between the two. You can do this by creating a chart or writing a report. Where can you find a whale or dolphin? A trout or catfish? How many ways can we protect these valuable bodies of water? You can even draw pictures to go with what you've learned.

How Deep Is the Ocean?

You may already know that the world's highest mountain is Mount Everest, measuring an enormous 29,028 feet. But did you know that there is a place in the Pacific Ocean where the water is so deep that Mount Everest would be covered completely if it was moved there? That place is called the "Mariana Trench," and the water is 36,198 feet deep!

PRESERVING NATURE'S RESOURCES

Do you recycle? Do you know what causes acid rain? Do you know why some animals and plants are endangered? In this chapter you'll learn about some great craft projects that will show how much you care about the earth. You can help others learn what they can do to protect the earth's precious resources. What you help preserve today will be around for others to enjoy tomorrow.

YOUR OWN WORLD

319

A diorama is a 3-D model of an area. Making a diorama is a good way to learn about a part of nature—and show what you've learned.

What You'll Need: Reference books, shoe box, markers or paint, craft glue, nature decorations, clay, cotton balls, scissors

The world is made up of many different types of habitats or environments. To create your diorama, you'll first need to learn about one kind of habitat. You might pick the desert, woods, or someplace else. Learn about the plants and animals that live there, the different kinds of rocks and water sources, and anything else that makes that habitat unique.

Once you have a picture in your mind of what the area is like, turn that picture into your diorama. Turn the shoe box on its side. On the sides and "roof" of the box, draw or paint the background of your habitat. Use what is the "floor" of the shoe box to make the foreground of your diorama. You might glue down sand and rocks for a desert, or toy trees and a "lake" (shallow cup of water) for a woods. Make plants and animals out of clay to populate your habitat. Glue cotton balls to the top of the box in order to put clouds in the sky.

MINI-ECOSYSTEMS

320

For a science project—or just for fun—make a display of the world's forests, deserts, and grasslands.

What You'll Need: Aquarium or gallon glass jar, potting soil, sand, charcoal for house plants, purchased or collected plants

"Biomes" are large areas of the earth that are determined by the plant communities that grow there. You can re-create the six major biomes of the earth in miniature using terrariums. Clean and dry an aquarium or gallon jar. Pour a ½-inch layer of charcoal in the bottom, then add about four inches of potting soil. (For a desert use a mixture of ½ potting soil and ½ sand.) Buy your plants, or ask someone for permission to collect plants from their property or garden. Never collect plants from nature, because they could be endangered. Here is a list of biomes and some suggestions of plants you can use:

Tundra (such as Northern Canada and Alaska): lichens, mosses, and any of the small alpine plants sold for rock gardens. These will need a sunny window.

Northern coniferous forest (such as Southern Canada, Northern U.S.): Piggyback plants and small ferns.

Deciduous forest (such as Eastern U.S.): Violets, Wintergreens, strawberries, and small ferns.

Grassland (such as the Midwestern U.S.): Plant a prairie wildflower seed mix that includes several grasses.

Desert (such as the American Southwest): Purchase cacti or aloe vera plants. Don't overwater or overfertilize. Leave the lid off.

Tropical Rain Forest (such as the Amazon Basin): Most common houseplants come from the tropics. Try African Violets, Creeping Charlies, or Aluminum Plants.

WHAT IS SMOG?

The word "smog" was created in 1905, and is a combination of the words "smoke" and "fog," the two main ingredients in smog. (Chemicals from pollution are also in smog.) Smog darkens the skies and pollutes the air. It is common in large cities, and can be a serious threat to plants and animals.

BE AN ECO-SCIENTIST

321

An "eco-strip" is a small strip of land that is part of an ecosystem. Create your own eco-strip.

What You'll Need: Sticks or large rocks; field guides to rocks, plants, and animals; notebook; pen; markers

You can make an eco-strip by marking off a section of land with sticks or large rocks. Choose a place such as a park, forest, beach, or other natural area. Then, study every detail of your eco-strip. This is a fun activity to do with a friend, because each of you will notice different things.

Use field guides to help you identify rocks, plants, and animals; record your findings in a notebook. Identify as many of the eco-strip's plants, animals, and rocks as you can. Look for signs of animals, such as tracks. Also look for ways in which humans have affected the eco-strip in good or bad ways. Maybe hikers have left trash, or maybe people have put out a basin of water that animals need in hot weather. Take notes about everything you observe. Finally, make a detailed map of the eco-strip.

RAIN, RAIN—GO AWAY

322

Sometimes chemicals get in the air and mix with water to form "acid rain."

What You'll Need: Water, vinegar, two jars, sod

Put ¼ cup of water in one of the jars. Ask an adult to cut two small squares of sod from your lawn or buy some sod at a nursery. Push one square of sod down into a jar so that the sod's soil is in the water. Then put ¼ cup of vinegar in the other jar. Push the second square of sod down into the jar, so the soil is in the vinegar. Now place both jars in a warm, sunny place, and watch what happens over the next several days. Vinegar is an acid, like the acid in acid rain.

Acid rain is a worldwide problem. It can be caused by smoke from factories, burning coal, and even car exhaust. In addition to harming plants, acid rain also pollutes bodies of water, kills fish, and destroys rocks and buildings!

"DON'T GO!"

323

Endangered animals are animals that are in danger of becoming extinct. Find out how to help these vanishing creatures.

What You'll Need: Reference books, poster board, markers

There are more than 700 species of animals on the endangered list, including the giant panda, the blue whale, and the bald eagle. Do research to find out some of the other animals that are facing extinction. (Local nature organizations or local zoos are good places to ask.) Then, choose one endangered animal that you especially care about. Learn as much as you can about that animal. Find out where it lives, why it is endangered, and what people are doing to help (and maybe to harm!) it. Most important, find out what you can do to help.

Here's one thing you can do: Make a poster telling others about the animal and how they can help. Try to display your poster in a public place—such as a library or store—where lots of people will see it.

SAVING THE ANIMALS

An endangered species of animal is one that is in danger of dying out. This danger could be because hunters kill off the animals, or it could be because the animal's environment has changed. People can help reverse the situation, though. In 1965, only 6,000 vicunas—a camel-like animal that lives in South America—were still alive. People killed vicunas for their wool. By protecting the vicuna from hunting, and by giving them an appropriate place to live, there are now about 160,000 vicuna today.

HARD-WORKING ANIMALS

324

Animals help people in so many ways! How many can you think of?

This activity is fun to do with a friend!

Name any animal. Then have a friend list the many ways that animal can help people. When your friend is done reciting, see if you can think of any additional ways. Have your friend pick the next animal, so you can recite the list.

For starters, think of what kinds of animals live on farms and ranches. What about companion animals such as seeing-eye dogs? You can make this a game by writing down separate lists, then comparing them. Who can think of the most?

325

MYSTERY BOXES

Challenge your friends to discover—by touch only—what lies in your mystery boxes!

What You'll Need: Shoe boxes, tape, scissors, paper or fabric, nature objects, index cards, pen

For each mystery box, tape the lid onto a shoe box and cut a hole in one end large enough to put your hand through. Cover the hole with paper. Cut eight slits from one side of the paper to the other in a star shape, so that you can put your hand in but the hole will still be covered. Instead of cutting some paper, you could hang a small piece of fabric in front of the hole on the inside, forming a curtain.

Now put your mystery object inside the box. Remember that your friends trust you, so only use objects that won't harm them or make them feel bad in any way. Try shells, rocks, driftwood, leaves, twigs, or cones. Make up a riddle or a poem to go with each object. Write it on a card and put it on the box. Then decorate the box.

Let your friends put a hand through the hole and try to guess what the object is. After everyone has made a guess, let someone take the object out for all to see.

A TRAGIC LESSON

326

Oil spills are a terrible tragedy for all of nature. See how they affect animals

What You'll Need: Two ice cubes, two sealable plastic bags, three plates, four cotton balls, vegetable oil

1. Put an ice cube into each of the plastic bags. Squeeze all the air out of the bags, and seal them. Put each of the bags on a plate.

2. Soak two cotton balls in vegetable oil. Put one of the cotton balls on top of one of the plastic bags. Make sure the cotton ball stays on top of the ice cube. Put the other oil-soaked cotton ball on an empty plate.

3. Put a dry cotton ball on the other plastic bag (on top of the ice cube). Put another dry cotton ball on the empty plate next to the oil-soaked cotton ball.

4. Let everything sit for 20 minutes. Pick up the two dry cotton balls—the one that is on the ice cube, and the one that isn't. Are they about the same temperature, or is one colder? Then pick up the two oil-soaked cotton balls—the one that is on the ice cube, and the one that isn't. Does one feel colder? Finally, pick up the two cotton balls that are on the ice cubes. Does one feel colder? What does this tell you about the connection between oil and keeping warm?

Imagine that those cotton balls are birds, otters, or other animals. When an animal gets soaked with oil, it gets cold, just like the oil-soaked cotton balls. That's because oil destroys the natural insulation that animals have.

Whenever there's an oil spill, animals die for many reasons. Some are poisoned by the oil. Birds starve to death because they cannot fly to catch food. Some animals die because their food has been killed by the oil. And some animals freeze to death because oil has destroyed their ability to stay warm.

CLEANING UP

Oil spills threaten humans, animals, and the environment. It is important to begin cleaning up an oil spill as quickly as possible. Clean-up crews often place long plastic or rubber barriers around the spill, so it cannot spread further. They may try to vacuum up the oil, using special machines. They also may try to absorb the oil, using spongelike pads.

SOUNDS OF NATURE

327

Understand how different parts of nature work together by learning to recognize the components.

What You'll Need: Paper, pens

This is the perfect outdoor activity to do with a friend on a lazy summer day.

Go outside, find a comfortable place to sit down, and close your eyes. (Try not to fall asleep.) Pay close attention to the sounds you hear. Do you hear birds? the wind? crackling leaves? After about five minutes, write down all the sounds you've heard. Then compare lists. See if you or your friend heard something the other one missed.

328

UNDOING POLLUTION

We all know some things that cause water pollution. In this experiment, you'll learn just how hard it is to undo pollution.

What You'll Need: Bucket, water, pollutants (dirt, oil, trash), tongs, strainer

Fill a five-gallon bucket with clean water. Now, do your best to pollute the water. Throw in dirt, gravel, vegetable oil (to stand for toxic oil spills), trash (plastic packaging and any other kind of trash you've seen polluting water in nature), and other kinds of pollution. Yuck!

Now, here's the hard part: What can you do to un-pollute the water? You can use tongs, strainers, and anything else you can think of. Can you get the water really clean again?

329

DON'T THROW IT AWAY!

If you and your family aren't recycling yet, now is the time to start! Set up your own recycling center.

What You'll Need: Cardboard boxes, marker

Recycling is one of the best things you can do for nature—and for people. Recycling saves trees, energy, and many other resources that we all need. And recycling helps reduce the amount of pollution and trash in the world.

To start your own recycling center, find out what items can be recycled in your area. (Call city hall or your local newspaper.) Then find out where items to be recycled can be dropped off—or if they can be picked up at your home. It's easy to set up a center at your home so everybody will remember to recycle. Simply put cardboard boxes next to the trash can, and label them: "Newspapers," "Aluminum Cans," and "Glass Containers." These are the items that are most commonly recyclable. In some areas, you can also recycle some kinds of plastic.

RECYCLING FACTS

While the problem of pollution can seem overwhelming, there are solutions. Paper can be recycled after the ink is removed by a special process, and steel and aluminum cans can be melted down to make new cans. When making glass items, old glass can be added to new glass. This mixture needs a lower temperature during creation, so less energy will be needed.

WHAT'S IT GOOD FOR?

330

Everybody knows that recycling is one good way to help nature. But there's another way, too: Reuse.

What You'll Need: Plastic milk jug, scissors

"Recycling" means saving things so they can be turned into new products. "Reusing" means using products in new ways, instead of throwing them away. For instance, a plastic milk jug is a product that can be reused in many ways. Here are some ideas:

• Make a watering can for flowers. All you need to do is have an adult cut off the top of the jug, above the handle.

• Plastic milk jugs with the tops cut off make great organizers for craft supplies. Use them to store your nature finds until you're ready to use them.

• Milk jugs are also good containers for sprouting seeds. Have an adult cut the top off to make a flower pot. Then poke holes in the bottom for drainage. You can get your summer vegetables or flowers started inside and transplant them outdoors when the weather gets warmer.

• Make a "drinking fountain" for small wild animals by cutting the jug to make a shallow tray.

Can you think of other products that you could reuse, instead of throwing them away? Each time you go to throw away a package or other product, ask yourself, "How could I use this again?"

WATER CONSERVATION

How much water do you think you use each day? A gallon? 20 gallons? Believe it or not, the average person uses 100 gallons of water a day! We use 5-10 gallons a minute just to take a shower, and another gallon each time we brush our teeth. Since nature only has a limited amount of water, we all need to be careful that we don't waste our precious water supply—even if that means taking shorter showers.

PAPER MAKING

Recycle your old paper and make new, unique paper that you can't buy in any store!

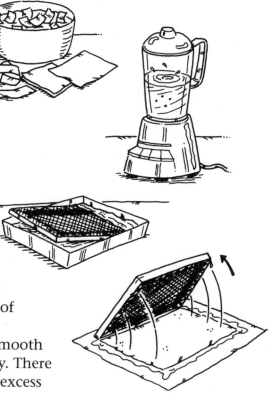

What You'll Need: Stiff wire screen; old paper; bowl; water; blender; dish pan or roaster pan; rags or tea towels (use smooth cloth, not terry cloth); iron

Recycling paper at home is fun and easy, but a little messy! Do this in the kitchen and have a lot of towels ready for clean-up.

1. With the help of an adult, bend the sharp edges of the wire screen over and flatten them. You can also make a wooden frame and staple the screen onto it.

2. Tear white scrap paper into small pieces and soak them in a bowl of warm water.

3. Put the soaked paper in the blender with equal amounts of water and blend until mushy. Do not fill the blender more than half-full. If you have a lot of pulp, blend it in batches.

4. Pour the pulp into the dish pan or roasting pan. Add a gallon of warm tap water. You should have a thin slurry of paper pulp.

5. Tilt the screen away from you and dip it into the pan with a smooth motion. Hold it level under the water, then lift slowly and smoothly. There should be an even layer of pulp on the screen. Tilt the screen to let excess water run off.

6. Let the pulp dry a bit. Then lay a soft, absorbent towel or rag out on a table and quickly flip the screen over onto it. Blot the back of the screen with another rag to absorb excess water. Gently peel the screen from the sheet. This process of blotting and removing the fresh sheet is called "couching" (pronounced "cooching").

7. Let the paper air-dry, or place another cloth over it and have an adult iron it dry and flat. Peel it away while still damp so it doesn't fuse to the cloth. Save the leftover pulp by freezing it, or throw it away, but never pour it down the sink or flush it down the toilet!

NATURE'S RECYCLER

332

Mother Nature recycles everything. Nature will even help you recycle your garbage, turning it into fertilizer called "compost."

What You'll Need: Plastic garbage can; heavy-duty scissors or shears; dry leaves, grass clippings, or straw; vegetable matter; rake; plant mister

To make your own composter, cut some holes in a garbage can. Put the garbage can outdoors in a place where animals won't get into it. Put in a layer of dry leaves, grass clippings, and/or straw. On top of that dry layer, you can start adding food scraps. Vegetable and fruit scraps make great compost. (Just don't put in any meat scraps or coffee grounds!)

Every few days, use a small rake to mix up your compost, then moisten it with a plant mister. Doing these things will help nature recycle your garbage faster. You can also keep adding more grass clippings and leaves. It will take one to four months to turn your garbage into fertilizer, depending on things like the temperature and humidity. Then you can use the fertilizer to help plants grow in a garden.

VANISHING FISH

At one time, there was more than enough food in the oceans for everybody to eat. But, as fishermen have caught more and more fish, they have had to find new places to catch them. About 110 million tons of fish are caught each year, and many prized fish are disappearing. As the fish are vanishing, so are many other forms of water life, such as certain types of turtles and whales that survive on fish as their food source.

BOTTLE TERRARIUM

333

Recycle old pop bottles by turning them into habitats for houseplants.

What You'll Need: 2-liter soda bottle with black plastic base, scissors, plants, potting soil, charcoal (the best kind comes already crushed and bagged for houseplants).

First remove the black plastic base from the bottom of your soda bottle and set it aside. This will be the bottom of your terrarium. Use scissors to cut off the top of the bottle just below the "shoulder" of the bottle. When turned over, the bottle forms a clear dome over your terrarium.

Now sprinkle about ½ inch of crushed charcoal in the bottom of the black plastic base. Fill the base with potting soil up to about ½ inch from the top. Plant some small houseplants, woodland plants, seeds, or cuttings in the base. Water them until the soil is moist but not soggy. Cover the plants with the clear plastic dome you made from the rest of the bottle. Place your bottle terrarium in a sunny spot and water it regularly.

If you collect wild plants or seeds for your terrarium, be sure to collect on private property with permission only. Never collect plants from parks, state lands, or federal lands.

CLEAN UP YOUR WORLD

334

Nature has at least one thing in common with your room: It gets dirty.

What You'll Need: Rubber gloves, trash bags, group of friends, scissors

Some thoughtless people throw trash on the ground. Or sometimes trash ends up in nature by accident, like when the wind picks up your homework (or your mom's newspaper) and blows it away.

You and your friends can organize a clean-up day to get nature looking its best. Just pick an area that needs cleaning, such as an open field, a backyard, or a beach. Wear rubber gloves to protect your hands from germs and scratches, and collect trash in plastic garbage bags. Also watch out for sharp objects. If you find any hazardous waste, such as motor oil or old car batteries, report it. (If you're not sure who to call, call the police non-emergency number.) Your clean-up will do more than just make the area look better. It will actually make it safer for animals, plants, and people.

KNOCK ON WOOD

335

Trees give us more than just a shady spot on hot summer days. Find the products that trees provided.

Do you have a baseball bat? How about a pencil? Does your home have a wooden table or chairs? There are so many things made from trees it's hard to count them all! Try to walk around your house and find as many things as you can that came from trees. Look for wooden items, as well as paper and cardboard. Don't forget to count fruit—such as apples—that grow on trees.

SPEAK YOUR MIND

336

Voice your opinion about something in nature that you really care about.

What You'll Need: Stationery, pen, envelope, stamp

Are you concerned about stray animals? Air pollution? The destruction of the rain forest? No matter where you live, you have people who represent you in government. Each area of the United States has two senators and at least one congressional representative. The job of these people is to listen to the people in their area, and try to do something about their problems and concerns. So, why not write them a letter and tell them what's on your mind!

Be as specific as you can about what's bothering you. Tell them what you're doing to help and what you'd like them to do. Maybe they could try to get new laws passed to take better care of nature. You can even write to the President of the United States! After all, he's your leader, too.

Another way to make your voice heard is to write a letter to the editor of your local newspaper. Every newspaper has a page where it prints letters from readers. Many people read these letters, so it's a chance to tell a lot of people how you feel. Here are the addresses of your government officials:

(Your U.S. Senator's Name)
U.S. Senate
Washington, DC 20510

(Your U.S. Representative's Name)
U.S. House of Representatives
Washington, DC 20515

(President's Name)
The White House
1600 Pennsylvania Avenue
Washington, DC 20500

WHAT'S YOUR GAME?

337

It's fun to create your very own nature board game and play it with your friends.

What You'll Need: Poster board, index cards, markers, small stones or coins, dice

It may seem hard at first to make up a board game about nature. To get started, choose a theme such as "save the forest," "clean up that oil spill," or "recycle for life."

Then get out a board game that you like to play. You can use this game as a model for yours. Draw squares about the edges of your game board as shown and think of things to write or draw in the squares. Remember, everything in the game should be about nature. For example, you could have a player lose a turn for throwing trash in a river, or move ahead for picking up trash. Use your imagination!

Be sure to write down rules for your game. Again, use the rules from one of your games as a guide. Finally, try playing your game. You may find there are things you need to change. Keep working on it until your game goes smoothly!

COUNT ME IN

338

There are many organizations that exist to help take care of nature. Start a nature group of your own.

Some nature organizations focus on animals, while others turn their attention to saving the rain forests or mountains. Get a group of friends together to start your own organization. Ask a librarian about the different nature organizations. You may want to write to several groups and ask them to send you information about what they do. The organization will also tell you about things you can do to help nature. Then you can choose a focus for your nature group.

Once your organization is formed, get together once a week or once a month to do things that will help you learn about and assist nature. You can even design a nature newsletter (see next page) to keep everyone in your neighborhood informed.

NATURE NEWS

339

After trying out a lot nature activities, share your discoveries with others.

What You'll Need: Paper, typewriter or word processor, notebook, pen

If you have a typewriter or computer at home, you can use word processing and page layout programs to arrange your newsletter just like a real newspaper and add pictures. If you don't have either, you can still make your newsletter by hand on paper, using your neatest handwriting. Draw pictures or take photographs to paste onto the newsletter. You can "publish" your newsletter once a week and post it on your refrigerator, or make photocopies for your friends.

How do you get stories to write about? Go out each day to observe what's going on outdoors. Take a notebook with you and write down what you see. As a reporter, remember to record "who," "what," "where," "when," "how," and "why" for any event. Here are some sample headlines to give you ideas:

- Bird's Nest Found in Neighborhood Tree
- First Rose Sighting of the Spring
- The Jones Family puts up Bird Feeder

TAKING CARE OF NATURE

340

It's important to learn how all the parts of the environment fit together.

What You'll Need: One or more books about the environment

All the parts of nature together are often called the "environment." It's important to know how you fit in with the environment, and what you can do to help keep the environment healthy and beautiful. Read a book to learn about the environment. After you learn more about the environment, come up with an activity that will help it. What can you do?

GIFTS FROM NATURE

Holidays and birthdays are great times for decorating and gift-giving. Of course, you don't really need a reason to give the gift of nature! And the best gifts are homemade. Try your hand at some of the wonderful crafts in this section. What could smell better than a garland made from real greenery? Or look nicer than homemade wrapping paper? Natural decorations can be ecological, too, if you are careful about collecting your materials.

341 · PINE CONE TREES

It's easy to turn ordinary pine cones into these unique sparkly decorations!

What You'll Need: Large pine cones, shiny glass or plastic beads (about ¼ inch in size), craft glue, tweezers, glitter, paper plate or disposable dish

Gather large pine cones outdoors. Clean off any dirt or leaves. If the cones are closed, ask an adult to dry them in a warm oven until they open.

For beaded "trees": Set the cones upright on newspapers. Pour some white glue in a small dish. Hold a bead with a pair of tweezers and dip in the glue. Stick the bead on one of the cone bracts. Keep gluing beads on the cone until it is covered. Allow to dry.

For glittery "trees": Pour white glue into one paper plate and glitter into another. Roll the cone in glue first, then glitter. Allow to dry.

Now make winter scenes with your trees. Set them on a sheet of cotton or quilt batting and add some figurines. You can even use a mirror for a frozen pond and put your trees around it!

EVERGREEN GARLAND

342

Brighten your home with a fragrant garland made from evergreens.

What You'll Need: Evergreen sprigs (trimmings from a Christmas tree, or blown-down branches), rope, string or floral wire, ½-inch wide red ribbon, two-inch wide red ribbon, holiday lights (optional)

Gather twigs and branches of fir, juniper, or other evergreens. A walk in the woods after a heavy wind should yield plenty of material lying on the ground. Cut the greenery into 6-inch lengths.

Lay a few twigs alongside a rope at one end with the cut ends of the twigs pointing away from the end of the rope. (Your rope should be the length you wish your garland to be.) Wrap tightly with floral wire or string. Lay a few more twigs on the rope, overlapping the twigs that were tied on. Wrap with more wire. Keep going until the whole rope is covered with greenery.

Next, tie a ½-inch wide red ribbon to one end. Wrap the ribbon in a spiral around the garland and tie off at the other end. Tie large bows of two-inch wide red ribbon and attach to both ends of the garland to cover up the rope ends. You can use holiday lights to brighten your garland.

WRAP IT UP!

343

Create gift wrap using pressed flowers and recycled brown paper bags.

What You'll Need: Brown paper bag, scissors, iron, tape, craft glue, water, glass pan, spatula, pressed flowers and leaves (see page 75), tweezers, waxed paper

Cut the bottom off of a brown paper bag and cut it open along the seam. Spread the paper out flat. Wrap your package in the brown paper with the unprinted side out. Now pour a puddle of glue into a glass pan. Add a few drops of water and mix with a spatula. Add enough water to make the glue slightly runny.

Pick up one of the pressed flowers or leaves with tweezers. Dip it in the thinned glue, then lay it on the side of the package. Place a piece of waxed paper over the flower and rub all over to press the flower onto the paper. Decorate the sides with more flowers and leaves. Allow to dry completely.

POMANDER BALLS

344

These traditional spicy-smelling pomanders make great holiday decorations or gifts.

What You'll Need: Small oranges or apples, marking pen, nut pick or toothpick, whole cloves, ground spices, saucer, ribbon

Select a small, firm apple or orange without bruises. Be sure it is a small one, no more than three inches across. (Larger pomanders take a very long time to make and may not dry well.) Use a marking pen to divide the surface up into sections.

Working one section at a time, use a nut pick or toothpick to poke a hole in the skin. Stick the stem of a whole clove into the hole. Do not poke a lot of holes in the skin and then insert the cloves. Go one at a time so you can see how to fit the cloves together. Be patient. Fill one section at a time, allowing gaps between the cloves. The fruit will shrink as it dries, so the gaps will close up.

When the whole fruit is covered, pour ground cinnamon, cloves, nutmeg, or allspice into a saucer and roll the pomander in it. Allow the pomander to dry in a warm place for two weeks. Tie ribbons around it and hang up in the kitchen, or give as a holiday gift.

A NUTTY IDEA

345

There are many different sizes and shapes of nuts. Use a variety to make this lovely nut wreath.

What You'll Need: Wreath base (vine or cardboard), nuts (with shells), craft glue, decorations

Use a vine wreath (see page 107) or a cardboard ring as a base for a nut wreath. Glue nuts in the shell to the wreath. (You can use nuts you find, or nuts you buy at the store.) Add other decorations, such as sprigs of evergreen or red bows.

STRAW STARS

346

This easy-to-make garland shines naturally in the glow of holiday lights.

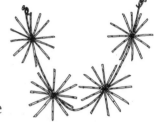

What You'll Need: Natural straw, string or colored crochet thread, scissors

First, cut a length of string a few feet longer than you want your garland to be. Next, soak the straw in water for five or ten minutes before using. Take six pieces of straw and cut them all to the same length. Hold in a bundle. Tie one end of the string tightly to the middle of the straw. The ends of the straw will spring out into a star shape. Cut more straw and make another star six inches to one foot down the string from the first one (depending on how big your stars are). Keep going until your garland is as long as you want it. Tie a loop on either end of the garland, and hang up on a wall away from candles or other open flames.

You can make more colorful garlands if you use colored crochet thread, which you can buy by the ball at a crafts store. Use red or green for Christmas garlands. Blue also looks nice.

WILLOW WREATHS

347

Use weeping willow branches or pussy willows to make lovely wreaths.

What You'll Need: Willow branches, string, ribbon, decorations

Ask permission from the owner of the willow tree to cut some branches. When the leaves fall from the willow, have the owner help you cut about 15 of the long, slender branches, each twice as long as you want the wreath to measure around.

Bend one branch to make a circle of the right size. Wrap the long end of the branch around itself, spiraling around the circle. Add more branches, and continue the spiral. As best you can, lay each new spiral alongside the old one. Keep going until you have used up all the branches you cut. Tie string around the wreath in four places to hold the branches in place. Set the wreath aside to dry for two weeks.

When dry, cut off the string and wrap the wreath in ribbon, spacing each turn of the ribbon a few inches apart. End with a large bow. Decorate the wreath with natural decorations such as pine cones, acorns, or dried flowers; or use bright Christmas balls, wooden cutouts, tiny toys, or other ornaments suitable for the season.

348 GUM SWEET GUM

The seed pods of the sweet gum tree are really unusual—and they can become glittering decorations.

What You'll Need: Sweet gum pods, styrofoam wreath base or cone, toothpick, gold or silver spray paint, ribbon

You can collect the spiky sweet gum tree balls under the trees in the fall. Most sweet gum trees make these balls in abundance! Always check first with the owner of the tree before picking them up. Spread them out on newspaper and let them dry for several days.

Now pick out a styrofoam base in the shape you want. You can choose a cone-shaped piece of styrofoam for a tree, circles for wreaths, balls, and lots of other shapes. Next, break a toothpick in half and stick it in one of the holes in a the sweet gum ball. Stick the other end into the styrofoam base. Keep going until the whole base is covered.

Lay your decoration on newspapers in a sheltered place outdoors or in a well-ventilated garage. Ask an adult to spray it with gold or silver spray paint. Put on 3 or 4 coats, allowing the paint to dry between coats. After the last coat, allow the paint to dry completely (at least 24 hours). Add a bow of red or green ribbon. Put one large bow on the wreath, or many tiny bows on the cone "trees." Set your decorations out to enjoy or give them as gifts.

SPICY DECORATIONS 349

These spice ornaments not only look good on your holiday tree, they smell good, too.

What You'll Need: Cinnamon sticks, ribbon, decorations (tiny pine cones, star anise, cardamom pods, holly berries, dried flowers), gold thread

Begin by gluing together a few cinnamon sticks. They should look like a small bundle of chopped wood. After the glue has dried, tie a bright-colored ribbon around the bundle. Then glue on tiny decorations such as other spices (star anise, cardamom pods), holly berries, tiny pine cones, or dried flowers. Let the glue dry. Finally, tie a gold thread around the bundle or just around the ribbon. Use the thread to hang the ornament.

350 LAVENDER BUNDLES

Sometimes these are called "lavender wands." Let their magical sweetness scent your clothes.

What You'll Need: Long stems of lavender, about four feet of ¼-inch wide ribbon for each bundle

This is a very old way of making sachets. Take 15 long spikes of freshly picked lavender. Tie them together right under the flower heads with the ribbon, leaving one end about ten inches long. Let this end remain inside the bundle. Now bend the stems gently back over the flower heads. Weave the long end of the ribbon carefully in and out of the stems until the flower heads are covered. Wrap the ribbon once or twice around the stems. Draw out the other end of the ribbon, which should now stick out between the stems, and tie the two ends together in a bow.

Hang the bundle up to dry thoroughly. When the bundles are ready, slip them into your dresser drawers to make your clothes smell sweet. Plenty of lavender may also help keep moths away, and it smells much nicer than moth balls! Lavender bundles also make nice gifts.

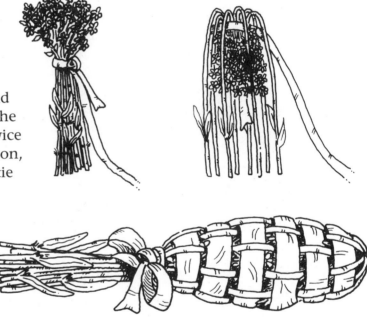

WHAT'S A MOONBOW?

While most people have seen a rainbow, how many have seen a moonbow? A moonbow occurs when three conditions are met: the moon will be full that night, it has just rained, and the moon has just risen. When all those conditions happen at the same time, a moonbow may appear.

BIRCH BARK VALENTINES

351

Make special Valentines out of natural treasures and your own verse.

What You'll Need: Thin birch bark (use only fallen or loose bark that is peeling off naturally), ink pen, natural object, scrap of ribbon

The paper birch is an unusual and delicate tree. Its waterproof white bark was used by Native Americans to make canoes. It can also be used like paper to make these valentines. Find a paper birch tree with thin strips of bark that have fallen or is already peeling off. Tear off only what you will use. Be careful not to tear off living bark—it could harm the tree!

Next, take a walk in a park, woodland, or other place where you can find early flowers, feathers, or evergreen twigs. With permission, collect a few natural treasures that you think are pretty. Lay your treasures out at home and let them inspire a Valentine poem. Evergreen twigs may make you think of a friendship that is "ever green." Flowers may stand for a blossoming friendship.

When you have composed your poem, write it on a piece of birch bark. Roll the bark around the feathers, flowers, or whatever objects you have used in your verse. Tie the Valentine with a ribbon and surprise someone on Valentine's Day—or any day!

Roses are red
Violets are blue
Some poems rhyme
Others don't

DECORATED EGGS

352

Using onion skins, create a natural dye for a different kind of Easter egg.

What You'll Need: Cheesecloth, one dozen eggs, leafy herbs (such as parsley or coriander), assorted onion skins (red, yellow, white), cotton string

Cut the cheesecloth into 6-inch squares. Take an egg in your hand and place an herb on the egg. Holding the herb in place, wrap a large onion skin around the egg. Place more herbs around the egg and wrap another onion skin around it. Place the covered egg on a square of cheesecloth. Tightly wrap the cheesecloth around the egg and tie it closed with a piece of cotton string. Repeat the process to make more eggs. Have an adult help you boil the eggs in water for 20 to 30 minutes. Take the eggs out of the water and allow them to cool. Unwrap the eggs and display them in a gift basket.

FLOWERS AGLOW

353

Use flowers you have pressed to make specialty candles.

What You'll Need: Column candles, paraffin, pan, paintbrush, pressed flowers (see page 75), tea lights

Start with a column candle. With help from an adult, melt some paraffin. Paint a thick layer of melted paraffin onto the side of the candle and quickly press a flower into the wet paraffin. The paraffin will work like glue to hold the flower to the candle. Paint another layer of paraffin over the flower, letting it drip between the flower and the candle. This will seal the flower. Put as many flowers on the candle as you like. You can also use feathers to decorate candles in the same way.

When the candle has burned enough that there is a 2-inch hole in the center of the column, put a tea light in the hole. Burn the tea light, instead of the column candle.

HOMEMADE HEARTS

354

These cinnamon hearts can be ornaments, garlands, or valentine greetings.

What You'll Need: Applesauce; cinnamon; white glue; rolling pin; heart-shaped cookie cutter; nail; spatula; cooling rack; string or ribbon; notecard, pen, and hole punch (optional)

Mix 1 cup applesauce, 1½ cups cinnamon, and ⅓ cup glue in a bowl. Form the mixture into a ball and chill it in the refrigerator for at least half an hour. (It's okay to leave it in the fridge overnight.)

Next, sprinkle some cinnamon on a cutting board. Roll out the dough until it is about ¼ inch thick. Cut out heart shapes with your cookie cutter. To make the hearts into ornaments or valentines, use a nail to make one hole in each heart. To make heart garlands, make two holes in each heart (one on each side). Use a spatula to move the hearts onto a cooling rack. Let them dry for about two days.

To make ornaments: Tie a string or ribbon through each heart.

To make valentines: Attach both a string and a Valentine greeting. You can write the greeting on a notecard. Use a hole-punch to make a hole in the Valentine so you can tie it to the heart.

To make garlands: Weave a long piece of ribbon through the hearts to connect them.

POTPOURRI

Sweeten your home with flowers and herbs the same way people have done for centuries.

What You'll Need: Scented garden flowers; paper towels; spices; glass container; ribbon; fabric, scissors, and spoon (optional)

Gather sweet-scented garden flowers early in the day after the dew has dried. Pick the petals off larger flowers, pick leaves off herbs, and spread the petals and leaves out to dry on paper towels. Smaller flowers may be dried whole. You can also cut the flower spikes from herbs such as lavender and dry them whole. Experiment to see which flowers keep their scent after drying. You may want to dry petals of colorful but unscented flowers to add color to your potpourri.

Next, blend your herbs and flowers together to make a pleasing scent. You can add spices such as cinnamon, nutmeg, or bay leaves. Try some of the following mixes, or make up your own combinations.

- Lemon verbena or lemon balm, lavender, and violets
- Rose petals, lavender, and bits of orange peel
- Pine needles, rosemary, violets, and bay leaves

Finally, put your mixture (called "potpourri") into glass containers with lids and decorate with ribbons.

To make sachets: Cut circles of fabric. Place a few spoonfuls of potpourri in the middle of the circle. Draw the fabric in over the potpourri and tie the bundle with ribbon.

LIFE ON EARTH

While there may be life on other planets, none has yet been discovered. Certain conditions must be met before there can be life, and the Earth meets them. The Earth travels around the sun in almost a perfect circle, causing temperatures to remain fairly stable. Also, we are just the correct distance from the sun to allow water to remain liquid. If we were closer to the sun, the water would evaporate, and if the Earth were farther away, the water would freeze.

HERB VINEGAR

356

Anyone who likes to cook will appreciate this special herb vinegar.

What You'll Need: Vinegar (cider vinegar, red wine vinegar, white wine vinegar, or balsamic vinegar are best), fresh cut herbs, glass bottles with stoppers or screw caps, masking tape, pen, index card, ribbon

Gather fresh herbs from the garden or buy them from the grocery store. Basil, thyme, sage, marjoram, tarragon, dill, or rosemary all work well. Wash the herbs gently in cool water to remove any traces of dirt. Scrub your bottles out well with soap and water, rinse thoroughly, and put upside-down in a dish rack to drain.

Fill the bottles with warm vinegar. Add several sprigs of any one herb to each bottle. Cap tightly and label your bottles with masking tape and a pen. Allow the bottles to sit for two weeks. Shake them a little every day while they're "brewing." At the end of two weeks, you can strain out the herbs and add fresh sprigs if you like, or leave old ones in if they still look nice. For a gift, remove the masking tape label. Decorate an index card to make a pretty label and tape to the bottle. Add a ribbon if you'd like.

HEALING HERBS

357

Many herbs are known for their relaxing and cleansing properties.

What You'll Need: Cotton or muslin bag (approximately 4"×3"), dried herbs, string or ribbon

An herbal bath bag is easy to make, and you can use it over and over again. Simply fill your bag with a mixture of dried herbs. (Some examples are listed below.) Then tie the top with a string or ribbon and make a loop at the top big enough to fit over a bathtub faucet. To use your bath bag, hang it from the faucet while hot water is running. (Make sure the bag hangs in the stream of running water.) You can also hang it in the shower. Let it dry completely before storing.

Herbs that help you relax: Chamomile, Lavender, Marjoram, Mint
Herbs that cleanse and deodorize: Sage, Thyme, Basil, Lovage
Herbs that relieve tired limbs: Bay, Bergamot, Hyssop, Meadowsweet, Rosemary

358

BEAUTY IN A BOTTLE

A sand painting in a bottle makes a nice gift. It's also fun to make a collection of them in different-size bottles.

What You'll Need: Bottle or jar, colored sand (available at crafts stores)

Start with a nice-looking bottle or jar that has a lid. Wide-mouthed jars are easier to work with than ones with narrow tops. Fill it with layers of different-colored sand to make a design.

Here are some ideas to try: Alternate thin layers and thick layers. Repeat color patterns. (For example, layer red, orange, yellow. Then repeat the pattern.) Or, tilt the bottle while you add sand. This will make wavy stripes. When the bottle is full, put the lid on. If you don't have colored sand, you can use different textures of sand (coarse and fine) or even sand and pebbles.

IT'S YOUR BEESWAX

359

Honey bees make beautiful beeswax honeycombs. Make attractive candles that have the color and texture of honeycombs.

What You'll Need: Sheets of beeswax, wicks (both available at crafts stores)

Honey bees make wax honeycombs to protect their queen's eggs from nature's elements. The wax is durable, waterproof, and can withstand most temperature changes. The bees also use the honeycombs to store honey or pollen for the cold winter months. It's easy to make beeswax candles. You can get sheets of beeswax (which are usually made from molded paraffin) and candle wicks at a crafts store. A 4"×6" sheet will make a small candle.

Measure out a length of wick a few inches longer than the width of the wax. Place the wick at one end of the wax. To hold the wick in place, roll the very end of the wax around the wick and press it tightly. Now roll the rest of the sheet of beeswax around a wick. When completely rolled, press the outside edge against the candle to keep it from unrolling.

POPCORN FRAME

360

The next time you make popcorn, save some for this fun frame!

What You'll Need: Popped popcorn (air-popped or microwave varieties work best), small matte self-standing picture frame, craft glue, colored pebbles or marbles

Be sure to let the popcorn cool before starting this project. Don't put butter or salt on it, either. First, glue a layer of popcorn around the edge of the frame. Let the glue dry, then glue some pebbles, marbles, or any other kind of colorful decorations on the frame wherever you want. Let the glue dry again, then fill in any remaining gaps with more popcorn.

LOOKS DELICIOUS!

361

You can use real fruit to help you make these lifelike papier-mâché sculptures.

What You'll Need: Fresh fruit, bowl, craft glue, water, paper towels, old newspapers, paintbrush, knife, acrylic paints, sealer

Start with a variety of fresh fruits such as bananas, apples, oranges, and pears. Pour some white glue into a bowl and stir in an equal amount of water to dilute it. Tear paper towels into 1-inch strips. You'll need a big pile of paper towel strips.

Cover your work space with lots of old newspaper. Begin pasting the paper towel strips onto the fruit. Hold a strip over the bowl of glue. Use the paintbrush to push the strip into the glue, wetting it on both sides. Then use the paintbrush to "paint" the strip onto a piece of fruit. Keep adding strips until the fruit is completely covered. Then repeat the whole process until the fruit is covered with four layers of strips.

Let the papier mâché dry completely. Have a grownup use a sharp knife to cut the fruit in half. Then remove the fruit from the papier-mâché shell. Use more papier-mâché to join the two halves of your papier-mâché fruit. When it's dry, paint the fruit with acrylic paints. You can make it look as much like real fruit as possible. Or, you can make wild and crazy-looking imaginary fruits.

When the paint is dry, seal the sculptures with at least one coat of acrylic sealer.

362 VINE-COVERED VASE

Natural vines add charm to any home. You can use any kind of jar or bottle to make a simple vase.

What You'll Need: Jar or bottle; smooth, flexible vines (such as honeysuckle, grape, or clematis) with leaves removed; scissors or pruning shears; craft glue

Put a line of glue around the middle of the jar and press the end of a vine into the glue. Press the vine firmly until it is held in place, then let the glue dry. Once the glue dries, you can wrap the vine tightly around the jar, working up from the middle to the top. Try to wrap the layers as close as possible to one another. If you get to the end of the vine before reaching the top, glue the end in place and start another vine. Once you reach the top of the jar, cut off the end with scissors or shears and glue it in place.

After you've done the top half of the jar, start at the middle again and wrap the bottom half the same way. Let the vase dry for two hours before using. You can decorate your vase with leaves, pebbles, or dried flowers.

OVER THE RAINBOW 363

You don't need to wait for it to rain in order to find this rainbow. Add some color to any plant.

What You'll Need: Clay flower pot (6 inches in diameter), craft glue, paintbrush, yarn (in the following colors: violet, blue, green, yellow, orange, red)

Wash the flower pot (even if it's new) with dishwashing detergent. Rinse thoroughly and place it in the sun to dry. Apply a one-inch band of glue around the base of the flowerpot. Wrap violet yarn around the flower pot, covering the band of glue. Apply another one-inch band of glue around the flower pot above the violet yarn. Wrap blue yarn around the pot. Continue gluing and wrapping colored yarn up the flower pot until it's covered completely. Let the glue set, then put a plant in the flower pot.

ROASTED NUTS

364

Nuts are full of energy-rich oils. That's why they're a favorite food of many forest animals—and us!

What You'll Need: Bag or bucket for gathering, long stick, mesh bag, nutcracker, cookie sheet, salt

Look for nuts in October and November. What kind of nuts you find depends on the area of the country you live in. In the east, you'll find hickory, beech nuts, and butternuts. In the west, you may find wild filberts (hazelnuts) or piñon pine. You may also find walnuts and black walnuts planted ornamentally just about anywhere.

The best time to go nutting is after a wind storm, early in the day before the squirrels have picked up too many. Take a long stick to help you reach nuts still on the branches. Small trees can be gently shaken to loosen nuts.

Let the nuts dry in the shell in a sunny place for a week or more. Hang them up in a mesh bag to store them. Roasting nuts brings out their flavor. To do this, crack them open with a nutcracker. Spread the meats out on a cookie sheet and sprinkle with salt. Roast in a 325°F oven for about ten minutes, stirring several times. Watch them carefully—take them out as soon as they turn brown, or they will burn. Fresh roasted nuts in a decorative tin makes a great gift for a "nutty" friend or relative.

BE A MILLIONAIRE

365

Money is no object with these coins created from natural clay. Or make a coin medallion or necklace as a gift.

What You'll Need: Natural or modeling clay, coin, nail, yarn (silver or gold), paint (optional)

Take a small amount of clay and use your palms to flatten and shape it into a coin. Now take a real coin and press it into the clay to make a design. Use different sized coins for larger or smaller clay coins. (You can also use a button or a ring to make an interesting impression.) Let your coins dry for about a week. Then paint them to look like real coins.

To make a medallion or necklace: Before your coin dries, make a hole in the top with a nail. Once it is dry, string silver or gold yarn through the hole. String several together to make a necklace.

INDEX